The
Right
Questions

The Right Questions

Ten Essential Questions to Guide You to an Extraordinary Life

Debbie Ford

HarperSanFrancisco

A Division of HarperCollins*Publishers*

FIRST EDITION
Designed by Joseph Rutt

Library of Congress Cataloging-in-Publication Data
Ford, Debbie.
The right questions : ten essential questions to guide you to an extraordinary
life / Debbie Ford.—1st ed.
p. cm.
ISBN 0–06–008627–0
1. Choice (Psychology) I. Title.
BF611.F67 2003
158.1—dc21   2002038794
03 04 05 06 07 RRD(H) 10 9 8 7 6 5 4 3

To my beloved father in heaven, the
Honorable Judge Harvey Ford,
who taught me the power and the potency
of asking the right questions.

Your wisdom lives on in my heart.

Contents

1 The Moment of Choice   1

2 Waking Up from Autopilot   22

3 Exposing Your Underlying Commitments   41

4 Will This Choice Propel Me Toward
an Inspiring Future or Will It Keep Me
Stuck in the Past?   60

5 Will This Choice Bring Me Long-Term
Fulfillment or Will It Bring Me
Short-Term Gratification?   69

6 Am I Standing in My Power or
Am I Trying to Please Another?   78

Contents

7 Am I Looking for What's Right or
Am I Looking for What's Wrong?   94

8 Will This Choice Add to My Life Force
or Will It Rob Me of My Energy?   104

9 Will I Use This Situation as a Catalyst
to Grow and Evolve or Will I Use It
to Beat Myself Up?   115

10 Does This Choice Empower Me or
Does It Disempower Me?   125

11 Is This an Act of Self-Love or Is It
an Act of Self-Sabotage?   136

12 Is This an Act of Faith or Is It an
Act of Fear?   148

13 Am I Choosing from My Divinity or
Am I Choosing from My Humanity?   157

14 Living the Answers   176

Acknowledgments   181

About the Author   183

1

The Moment of Choice

Every day, each of us makes a multitude of choices that will impact our lives. Some of these choices are minor and will only impact the next few minutes, hours, or days, while others will completely change the direction of our lives. Some choices are easy to make; some are more difficult. Some will lead us straight to success, while others will bring us face-to-face with failure. Some will seem earthshakingly important, while others will seem completely insignificant. But what's imperative for each of us to know is that, no matter how large or small, easy or difficult, each choice that we make, individually or collectively, alters the direction of our lives. The quality of our choices will dictate whether we will struggle in frustration or live an extraordinary life—the life of our dreams.

Our ability to make choices implies certain rights and freedoms. If we can choose, then we can determine which decisions we will make about our bodies, our health, our relationships, our finances, our careers, our social lives, and our spiritual beliefs. Choice allows us to pick, to select, to decide between paths. To go right or left. To move forward or backward, be happy or sad, loving or hateful, satisfied or discontent. Choice gives us the power to be successful or unfulfilled, to be good or great, to feel pleasure or pain. We can have chocolate or vanilla; we can work or play, save or spend, be responsible or be a victim. We can keep busy or slow down, be faithful or unfaithful, be disciplined or lazy. We can pursue a path that reflects our highest selves or one that reflects our lowest selves. Ultimately, we are the ones who get to choose.

What makes each of us special and distinguishes us from all other forms of life is our capacity to weigh our options and make conscious, deliberate choices. Choice might just be our most precious gift. When we were younger, we eagerly anticipated the moment when we no longer had to do what others told us. We saw our ability to choose for ourselves as a priceless gift. We anxiously waited for the day when we could get out from under years of our parents' rules and finally take control of our lives. We longed for the time when we could step out and become the masters of our own destinies, savoring that defining moment when we could decide when to wake up, when and what to eat, when to go to bed—or not. As young adults, the right to choose equaled freedom. Our ability to choose for ourselves unleashed the limitless possibility of creating a future filled with our dreams and desires. Choice offered us hope. It promised us an exciting life—a life where we were free to design and create whatever we pleased. As young adults we made choices because they were exciting, because they felt good, because they held the promise of satisfaction and gratification.

In our youth it's easy to say, "I'll make my dreams happen later" or "Next year will be my year." Youth affords us the luxury of believing that "one day" we will magically arrive at the destination of our dreams. But then something happens. Adulthood catches up with us and a sobering reality sets in: the day we've been waiting for will not magically arrive.

Our todays are based on the choices we made yesterday, and the ones we made three days ago, three months ago, and three years ago. We don't wind up fifty thousand dollars in debt because of one choice. We don't put on thirty unwanted pounds as a result of a couple of poor choices. And our relationships usually don't fall apart overnight because of one bad decision. We are where we are because of repeated unconscious or unhealthy choices that we've made day after day after day that add up to the reality we find ourselves in.

If we want to understand why and how we created our present reality, all we need to do is look at the choices we made in the past. Examining our present circumstances will show us that we got where we are as a result of decisions we made yesterday and the days before that. Likewise, if we want to know what our lives will look like in the future, we have to examine the choices we are making today. Maybe we've never considered our lives in this way. But the fact is that our futures are determined by the choices we are making right in this moment. So why, then, do most of us spend so little time really thinking about our choices? Why do we often fail to look both ways before we forge ahead, never considering all of our options and their consequences? Our lives are not a crapshoot, bad luck, or our parents', husband's, or boss's fault. Inherent in this fact is both good news and bad news. The bad news is that we are solely responsible for the condition of our lives. The very good news is that we and we alone have the power to change our lives, and we can choose to do so at any moment.

It's really quite simple: if we want our lives to be different, all we have to do is make different choices. Most of us continue to make the same choices out of habit, comfort, fear, or laziness and then wonder why we don't get different results. The truth is, we're so busy trying to survive life that we don't even realize that our choices and actions aren't translating into our hopes and dreams. We're too distracted with the "doingness" of our daily lives, so we take the easiest, most accustomed route or the path of least resistance, even if it leads us somewhere we don't really want to go. Many of us stumble through each day doing the best we can, without the awareness and the tools we need to change the course of our lives. Then we're shocked when we wake up and discover that we have been working toward the same goals and desires for years and still we aren't where we'd like to be in our lives.

Most of us have lost sight of the relationship between our choices, our actions, and their outcomes. Instead of taking responsibility for our current state of affairs, we become masters at assigning blame, pretending that everything is someone else's fault when our lives turn out not to be the wonderlands we want them to be. We may even point fingers at others instead of looking at the choices we've made that have landed us exactly where we are today. Without bringing conscious awareness to our choices, we can't help but repeat the patterns of our past.

THE RIGHT QUESTIONS

If you are going to reach your goals and create the life you desire, you will have to make new choices that will lead you to new actions. This book is your road map. The ten simple questions you will find within these pages—what I have chosen to call the "Right Questions"— will give you the power and inspiration to consciously create a life you feel good about, one choice at a time. They will help you to become aware of the important choices and their consequences. They will guide you and support you in making the right choices. And there you will find the most direct route to your dreams.

The Right Questions consist of ten powerful inquiries

designed to reveal what is motivating your actions. The answers to these questions will immediately clarify your thinking and support you in making the choices that are in your highest and best interest. They are deceptively simple but incredibly powerful and can be used in any situation or at any crossroads. Here, then, are the Right Questions:

- Will this choice propel me toward an inspiring future or will it keep me stuck in the past?

- Will this choice bring me long-term fulfillment or will it bring me short-term gratification?

- Am I standing in my power or am I trying to please another?

- Am I looking for what's right or am I looking for what's wrong?

- Will this choice add to my life force or will it rob me of my energy?

- Will I use this situation as a catalyst to grow and evolve or will I use it to beat myself up?

- Does this choice empower me or does it disempower me?

- Is this an act of self-love or is it an act of self-sabotage?

- Is this an act of faith or is it an act of fear?

- Am I choosing from my divinity or am I choosing from my humanity?

Why these particular questions? I once heard the motivational speaker Tony Robbins say, "Quality questions create a quality life." The quality of our lives is made up of the sum of all our decisions. To make quality decisions, we need to see clearly. Asking either-or questions heightens our awareness and clarifies the results that we can expect from our actions. When you ask these questions in the decision-making process, you immediately see whether the choice you are about to make is an expression of your light or your darkness, whether the choice comes from your vision and dreams or from your fears and doubts. These questions supply you with the wisdom you need to make what was previously unconscious, conscious, so that you can choose with all the power that comes from being fully aware.

UNDERSTANDING THE IMPACT OF OUR CHOICES

Our choices affect our mood and the way we feel about ourselves. They influence the quality of our relationships with ourselves, others, and the world. For every action there is an equal and opposite reaction; this is the law of cause and effect. No action goes unnoticed. We may fool ourselves into believing that our actions do not matter, particularly if we think no one will know or that no one is watching. But all of our choices impact our futures. If we look at the people who have made a great difference in the world, we see that they all made courageous choices. We see that they came to their decisions with clarity, certainty, and focus. They disciplined themselves to make the choices that were not always comfortable or easy. They took the actions that fed their life force, their purposes, and their dreams. Every time we make a choice that is inconsistent with our heart's desires, we are not only moving away from what we say we want in life but actually dampening our life force—that unique inner power that keeps us alive spiritually and physically.

When we ask the right questions and make the right choices, we feed our life force. Several years ago, during a weekend retreat led by Ammachi, an Indian woman who is a spiritual leader to many people around the world, I came to understand this life force as I never had before. I had been feeling totally exhausted, and I decided to take my son, Beau, with me to Amma's retreat with the intention of doing some deep inner work. I knew I needed to make some changes in my life, but I wasn't sure what was wrong, what I should do, or in which direction to head. A weekend of prayer and meditation seemed to be just the tonic I needed to get clear on what changes I should make.

When I arrived at the retreat I proceeded into a huge hotel ballroom. I sat down with the other several hundred retreat participants and began to meditate. It was difficult for me to concentrate. The truth was that I was so out of balance I couldn't sit still. Rather than rustle around inside, I began wandering through the grounds of the hotel. It felt so good to be outdoors. Listening to the birds sing and feeling the wind cross my face and hearing it brush through the trees were just what my soul longed for. Slowly I began to unwind and settle into the natural rhythm of the retreat. Then I noticed that everyone was moving outside for an early-evening meditation. I found a place on a bench and joined the others in the group.

As I closed my eyes and turned my attention to my breathing, I felt how shallow my breath was, and I could hear only a faint whisper of what I knew should be a strong, fluid flow of air. I relaxed further and gave myself permission to surrender all that I knew and all that I felt. My only prayer was to get out of my own way in order to receive the guidance that I knew was available for me in the presence of this divine woman and a group of other spiritual seekers. As I finally let go, a wonderful vision occurred. Inside my mind I saw Ammachi enter into my consciousness. I breathed in deeply to absorb the wisdom I was receiving, and I could feel my heart opening wide to the truth of her words.

In my meditation, I heard her say that I would not be able to continue to carry out my teaching if I did not make some major changes in my life. She told me that I was burned out, that I lacked the strength and vitality to keep up the fast pace I was living. And then she showed me an image that has forever changed my life. In my meditation, she pointed to my lower abdomen and said, "We each carry a flame. Your flame is very small. It's only a flicker." She said that the choices I was making were not feeding my internal fire but rather diminishing its strength. I then saw an image of a healthy flame. It was a bold, roaring fire. Its essence was strong, bright, and powerful, with the colors of gold, amber, and red. This healthy, vital internal flame was much different from the one I had just seen in myself, which was dim, short, and weak. My fire's essence was faint, timid, and tired. It looked like if I didn't feed it some logs it would go out soon. As I listened more deeply I heard what I believe today to be the most important information I have ever received.

Each of us has an internal flame that is the keeper of our life force. Each choice we make either adds to this force, making it stronger, igniting and feeding our flame, or diminishes the force, dampening our internal flame, reducing its power.

When our internal fire roars, we feel strong, powerful, and confident. We have the strength and courage to speak truthfully and the humility and clarity to ask for what we need. A healthy flame fills our minds with vision and inspiration and gives us the stamina to envision our dreams and go after them. When we nurture our internal fires we see with great clarity and act with undeviating focus. A strong flame propels us into higher states of consciousness, where self-love and emotional freedom reside.

When our flames are low, however, we are vulnerable, frail, and weak. We feel scared and apprehensive and are filled with worry and self-doubt. When our flames have not been cared for and fed, we hunger for things outside ourselves to make us feel better. We withhold our communications to others, fearing that we are not worthy of love and happiness. When our flames are low, we are skeptical and cynical. We worry that others will want something from us and we fear that we have so little to give. When our flames are weak we don't have the defenses to fight off disease, doubt, worry, self-loathing, addiction, or criticism. When our flames are low we look to others to feed our fires because we haven't fed them ourselves. A weak fire is needy and falls prey to the ongoing negative dialogues that permeate our minds.

What's important to know is that the size and the health of our flames also affect those around us. A small flame causes others to worry about it, just as we would feel compelled to tend a fire that is threatening to extinguish itself. A sputtering internal flame demands that we pay attention to it and look for ways to make it strong and revitalize it. Can we ever leave a weak fire unattended? Can we ignore it for more than a few minutes? Not if we want it to keep going. A small flame sputters and is always in danger of being extinguished, whereas a healthy flame stands tall and burns brightly, with enough power to sustain itself in a strong wind.

Our flames are our essence. When they are well fed, they hold all the power of that roaring fire. But our internal flames must be looked after and protected. We must honor them and care for them, tend them and nourish them, if they are to stay strong. Our job is to protect these flames, knowing that they are our life force, our spirit, and the keeper of our divinity.

Now I'll give you the sobering news: our choices inform our behaviors and our actions. Every choice we make either brings wood to our internal fires or sprinkles a little water on them, diminishing their power. If we wish to stand in all of our light, if we wish to express ourselves authentically, and if we want the power to bring our purpose to the world, our first commitment must be to keeping our internal fires—our life force—strong.

Now I'd like you to imagine that your only job in life is tending to that inner flame, keeping it vital and roaring. Imagine that there is absolutely nothing you need to do except make the daily, weekly, monthly, and yearly choices that will protect that flame. Imagine how you would care for that flame's power, knowing that it and it alone can give you all the love, money, health, security, fulfillment, and peace of mind that you desire. Most likely you would take very, very good care of that flame and make empowering, life-enhancing choices to keep your life force strong.

Here are some examples of choices that dim your light, and then some examples of those that make your flame strong and healthy.

Choices That Dim Your Light

- Being around people who criticize you and can't see your magnificence
- "Should"s
- "Have to"s
- Perceived obligations
- Trying to be nice
- Trying to get others' approval
- Withholding communication
- Lying to yourself

- Gossiping

- Being late

- Not caring about other people's feelings

- Comparing yourself to others

- Judging yourself

- Judging others

- Not taking the time to enjoy what you have

- Looking to others to make you happy

- Living in fear

- Withholding success from yourself

- Thinking that others are better than you

- Giving away your power

- Ignoring your deepest desires

- Overspending

- Overeating

- Overindulging

- Wasting your time

- Deflecting compliments

- Trying to be someone you are not

- Not setting strong boundaries

- Not having enough alone time

- Withholding love from your family

- Withholding acknowledgment from yourself

- Overexhausting yourself

- Ignoring your inner voice

Choices That Make Your Fire Roar

- Having empathy for others

- Taking time for yourself

- Spending time with those you love

- Noticing what you have done well

- Resting

- Having fun

- Playing

- Exercising

- Eating well

- Spending your money wisely

- Planning for the future

- Being with people who inspire you

- Taking time to nurture yourself

- Doing what's in the best interest of you and your community

- Appreciating yourself

- Being honest with yourself and others

- Honoring your word

- Paying your bills on time

- Being compassionate

- Being intimate with those you love

- Making love

- Doing charity work

- Telling others how much they mean to you

- Doing what you love

- Going after your dreams

- Making choices consistent with where you want to go

- Dancing

- Forgiving

- Taking responsibility

- Looking for what's good

- Looking for what's right

- Doing a job well

- Being present for your children

- Caring for your partner

- Listening to others from your heart

- Receiving others' love

- Empowering those around you

- Allowing others to contribute to you

- Creating a powerful support system

- Speaking your truth

- Saying no

FEEDING YOUR FLAME

How strong is *your* internal fire? Is it hearty, vital, spirited? Can it light up the sky? Does it light up those around you? Do people feel your presence, your flame, when you walk into a room? Or do you struggle every day trying to figure out how to be more successful, how to get more love, more money, a better body, more recognition? Do you try to maneuver the world to make your fire roar? Or do you bask in the warmth of your inner fire?

These are the questions you must ask yourself before we move forward. This is the time to tell the truth. Give yourself permission now to take a long, truthful look at your life and ask, "Am I who I want to be? Do I feel strong inside my body? Are the choices I make the choices of someone who has a roaring, healthy internal flame, or are they the choices of someone whose fire is tiring?"

We all need the warmth of our own and everyone else's fire. We need to know that each of our fires is well cared for and watched over. Nobody wins if even one of our internal flames goes unattended or, even worse, goes completely out.

2

Waking Up from Autopilot

In order to feed our internal flames, we must wake up and make each of our choices conscious. A conscious choice reflects our highest commitments and is in direct alignment with our vision for our lives. When we make conscious choices, we take into consideration the effect that our actions will have on our lives as a whole. We take the time to reflect on where our choices will lead us and the impact they will have on our future.

Every time we slip into unconsciousness and forget about our deepest desires, we fall into an automatic trance, collapsing into whatever programming and patterns exist from our past. This trance is like going on autopilot: it takes no effort, no thinking. It's the trance of denial.

This trance whispers in our ears, "It doesn't matter. Just one more time. I'll start tomorrow. I really don't want it anyway. It's okay; no one will know." The voice of this trance encourages us to take the easy way out. "No worries!" it cries as we turn off the road of our dreams and down the circular pathway of our past. The trance of denial takes us from one moment to the next, one day to the next, and one year to the next while our dreams and our lives turn into repetitive excuses taking us on the road to nowhere.

When we are acting on automatic, we fail to see the consequences of our behaviors. We blindly go about our days, never considering the long-term vision for our lives. We neither examine our motives nor try to understand what is directing our choices. Our actions are re-actions, our choices based on the way we feel in the moment, with no consideration for their impact on our future.

In any given moment we are being guided by one of two maps: a vision map, which is a deliberate plan for our future, or a default map, which is made up of our past. Choices made from our default map—our repetitive, automatic programming—do not nourish our flames, nor do they move us closer to our dreams. And even though they may feel right to us, they do so simply because they are familiar. Let me give you an example:

Jody, a pediatrician with a thriving practice, has a goal of taking one week off per quarter, for a total of four weeks' vacation time a year. Her assistant schedules these weeks well in advance on Jody's calendar. Yet whenever Jody gets backed up with patients, instead of looking to her vision map for direction, her automatic response, made from her default map, is to cancel her plans and take care of those in need. Many times she has given up her commitment to take time off for family and fun and acted unconsciously only to regret it in the end. Before Jody could grasp the freedom to do anything different, she first had to realize that her automatic response was guiding her actions. Her default map was directing her to say yes to the demands of her patients. Without looking, she made choices that ultimately took her away from the life she desired. Jody realized that when she was on autopilot she had no choice in this area of her life. This realization enabled her to make a new, conscious, choice that was in direct alignment with her goals and objectives.

When we're making unconscious choices, we can be certain that we are not present in the here and now.

don't have the energy." But on this particular day I stopped for a moment, closed my eyes, and asked myself a few of the Right Questions:

- "Will going to karate empower me or disempower me?"

- "Will going to class bring me closer to my desired future or keep me tied to the past?"

In an instant it became clear to me that, given my commitment to being a black belt by the time I'm fifty years old—three years from now—the only action to take was to put on my dobok and go to class. Once I became conscious, I was able to make a powerful, life-enhancing choice.

The question to ask is, If you loved yourself, if you believed you deserved to have what you wanted, why in heaven's name would you choose to take an action that would rob you of attaining your desired results? The answer to this question is simple. If you tell the truth you will probably discover that you have no choice in this area. You, with or without your knowledge, have been operating on automatic pilot, following your default map. When you act unconsciously, you unknowingly surrender to the trance of denial. You sacrifice your soul's dreams in exchange for comfort or instant gratification, powerless to stop taking a repetitive action with undesired consequences. In some instances, without realizing it, you can even head off at full speed in a self-sabotaging, opposite direction.

Whether you know it or not, you can always decide between conscious and unconscious choices. Every day you have the power to look away and assign your destiny to the wind or to move your life powerfully forward in the direction of your dreams. The Right Questions wake you up. This is not a dress rehearsal; this is your life. Either you will milk it for all it's worth and manifest what you truly desire or you will go to your grave regretting that you didn't make different choices. The Right Questions give you the opportunity to take yourself off autopilot and become the conscious navigator of your own reality. They will make you present to the truth and ground you in reality so that you can see whether or not your actions are in alignment with your goals. They will remind you that every time you make a choice, that choice either takes you closer to where you want to go or moves you further away.

CREATING YOUR FUTURE

Can you imagine taking off for a twenty-year road trip not knowing where you wanted to go? How would it feel to get into your car every day and just drive down whatever road looked good at the moment? Do you think that would inspire you? Is "destination unknown" an itinerary that would support you in jumping out of bed every day and becoming the greatest possible expression of yourself? If it would, read no further.

If, however, you think you might be overwhelmed by anxiety, frustrated, or bored to tears after a few days, months, or years of wandering aimlessly around the world, leaving your future to chance, then I invite you to stop right now and create a road map that will lead you to the destination of your dreams.

Having a vision, objectives, and goals supports us in knowing which choices we need to make. Our deepest desires emerge from our souls, inspiring us to evolve into what we are meant to be. Our goals guide us toward the roads we need to take. However, if we are unclear about our destination, we are easily misled. The longer we wander without purpose or direction, the more lost and unclear we become.

If you were planning a road trip across the country, would you leave without having a map? Or would you look at the map once and then forget about it? If that was your strategy, you might never arrive at your destination. But if you were absolutely committed to arriving at your destination in the shortest time possible, you would study the map carefully, charting out your route for each day. And if you made a wrong turn along the way, you wouldn't stop and spend five years beating yourself up. You would pull over, look at your map, and get back on track.

The most important thing you can do each day is to consult your vision map. The map is your vision of your life. It shows you where you are going. Without vision it's easy to fall prey to the heat of the moment and the whims of your habitual behaviors. Even if you begin your journey by setting small goals in different areas of your life, at least you will know in which direction to head. You need to revisit your goals, visions, and dreams in order to have a fixed reference point, a true north by which you can navigate and decide which steps you can take to bring your desires closer to becoming a reality.

Your vision acts as a reference point. Thus, it is essential to take a moment every day in which you focus on your vision and bring your goals into your conscious awareness. This process can be very simple. When you get up in the morning, before you begin your day:

- Take a moment of silence and meditation, and give yourself permission to have all that you desire.

- Tell yourself that it is safe for you to fulfill your heart's wishes.

- Remember where you want to go, why you want to go there, and what will be waiting for you when you arrive. Allow yourself to imagine how you will feel, how you will look, and how others will be inspired by you when your vision is fulfilled.

- Think about all the opportunities you will have during the coming day to make choices that support the fulfillment of your goals and dreams.

This daily practice will inspire you to make the highest choices for yourself throughout your day. Your vision will be fresh in your mind, and you will be clear about what you want. Then all you will have to do is ask the

Right Questions and you'll effortlessly know which choices to make.

When you keep your vision map in front of you, fleeting desires lose out to long-term commitments. If you're focused purely and intently on what you want, you'll be able to stand firm and make life-enhancing choices when you find yourself at a crossroads. Whether you're working on your career, your health, your relationships, getting sober, or being a better parent, you must keep your vision present. If you hold in your mind a firm picture of exactly what you want, you can determine whether the action you are about to take supports your goal. If you don't have your vision consciously in front of you, it will be impossible to make choices that are consistent with it. Taking a few moments to recall and become aware of your goals ensures that you won't be whisked away wherever the wind blows.

None of us are given visions for our lives that we can't fulfill— whether it's having a healthier body or a loving relationship or a more satisfying job or making a difference in the world. If we didn't have the ability to fulfill an authentic desire, we wouldn't have the desire in the first place. Our souls wouldn't yearn for the experience, and we wouldn't continue to long for it year after year.

ASKING THE RIGHT QUESTIONS
TO GET THE RIGHT ANSWERS

Recently, I used the Right Questions with my eight-year-old son. Beau didn't feel like doing his homework. He was in the middle of playing video games and was having so much fun he didn't want to stop. I knew that I could force him to do his homework, but I didn't want to reinforce his belief that homework is a drag. I really wanted to inspire him to see homework as something he wants to do. So I casually asked him, "Do you want to go to college?" He quickly said yes. I then asked, "Do you want to be as smart as your mom and dad when you grow up?" Again he said yes. Now he had a vision for his future in mind. When I asked him, "Will doing your homework bring you closer to your goal of going to college and being as smart as your mom and dad, or will it take you further away from that goal?" Beau's eyes widened and his face perked up.

I then asked Beau to imagine going to school the next day without having done his homework. "Would this choice make you feel good about yourself, or would it make you feel different, ashamed, or embarrassed?" It just took a moment for Beau to turn off his Nintendo and walk into the living room, where his homework was waiting. Beau chose to do his homework, not because I forced him, but because he clearly saw for himself that it was in his highest and best interest to do so.

In order to stay awake and be able to create a future that reflects our goals, we need to question the present. We need to question every choice we make and look at the positive or negative consequences of our actions if we are to align our daily actions with our deepest desires. In other words, once you have created a vision for your desired future:

- Keep your vision in your awareness.

- Consider your choices carefully before acting.

- Examine your past choices to see whether they have kept you on course or pulled you off.

- Ask the Right Questions to determine the most direct route you can take to arrive at the future you desire.

Most of us are waiting for the day when we'll do better, when we'll have everything we want, and when we will become the people we most want to be. But as you know, that day doesn't just magically arrive. That day is a choice.

The Right Questions will remind you of the life you long for and inspire you into it. But remember, making new choices can be uncomfortable. Turning around and heading west when you've been traveling east for six years is probably not going to feel comfortable. But after making a few right turns you'll find yourself back on the right track. Then you'll be able to relax and enjoy the journey toward the destination of your dreams.

BYPASSING THE INTELLECT

Often we can't see what is in our highest and best interest because our thinking process impairs our clarity. We spend much of our time and energy negotiating, rationalizing, and justifying our actions and our choices: "Should I do this?", "Should I not do this?" Asking the Right Questions takes all that negotiation and justification out of the process. The Right Questions leave us grounded in the truth and in the presence of our goals and desires. They bypass our intellects. Personally, I love the Right Questions because I am great at rationalizing and a master at creating excuses. I can reason myself out of anything. But now I try not to think. I just look at the results I desire and ask the Right Questions. When you ask, "Does this choice empower me?" the answer quickly emerges. You can't argue with it. Your mind might say, "I'm too busy; I'll start tomorrow." But all you need to do is ask yourself again, "Will this choice empower me? Will this action make my flame stronger?" If the answer is yes, then take the right action. Don't think about it; don't analyze it; don't justify it. We have all mastered the art of thinking our way to nowhere. We can dwell, ponder, and rationalize all we want. But if we wind up taking an action that leaves us feeling weak and disempowered, we have dimmed our flame, diminished our life force, and set ourselves back a couple of steps from our desired goals.

The truth is, most of us think too much. The answers we get from the Right Questions will inspire us to bypass our intellects and to act from our highest vision. When we take actions that feed our inner flames, we discover that there is really very little to think about. Then, having made the right choice, we will have the delightful experience of being at home in our bodies and at peace with our souls.

BYPASSING THE EMOTIONS

So many of our choices and decisions are also driven by our emotions. The three-, six-, or twelve-year-old inside us wants to make the choices and run the show. Asking the Right Questions gives us the ability to bypass our emotional states and take actions that support our goals, regardless of how we feel in the moment. There comes a time when we each need to bypass our automatic emotional responses and—instead of asking, "How do I feel about this?"—ask, "Will this choice bring me closer to my highest vision for myself?" In other words, our vision map, not our mood, should be our guide. Let's look at an example.

When you leave the house to go to the grocery store, you don't stop at every corner and ask yourself which way you *feel* like going. You know your destination, and you follow the directions. You probably even take the shortest route there. So why, when you are on your way to financial security, do you stop at every coffee shop or clothing store and ask, "Should I go in?" or "Do I feel like buying something today?" Why would you allow your emotions to determine whether you are going to fulfill your vision? Why not just follow the directions on your road map? If it says, "Financial freedom: No shopping for six months," why not just follow the route? If you were going to the grocery store you would take whatever the best route to get you there was, even if it didn't feel good at the moment, and you would follow it without consulting your feelings.

Maybe you've noticed: your emotions fluctuate constantly. Therefore, it's not the wisest idea to navigate by them. If you want to arrive at your desired destination, I suggest you forget about your emotions for a while. Save them for loving your children, for caring for the elderly, for making a difference in the world, for appreciating yourself. Don't use them as your compass to your future; they just weren't designed for that. As long as you look to your emotions to be your guide, you forfeit your right to achieve your goals.

Taking the high road and making the right choices may not always feel comfortable. In fact, it may feel very uncomfortable to make a choice outside the predictability and familiarity of your past. It might be painful not to go shopping, or to stay with your exercise program. If you do something different from what you've been doing for the past ten or twenty years, it will very likely feel scary. But once you can see that taking that action will leave you feeling empowered and strong, you can consciously decide which path you want to take.

To make conscious choices we must be willing to give up the quick fix, the feel-good moments, and surrender our attachment to doing things our way. We must stay present to our dreams and desires and bring awareness to our choices. The Right Questions are meant to stop us and make us think twice when we are about to take an action that is more consistent with our past than with our future.

The great news about using the Right Questions to achieve our desired results is that we don't have to feel good enough, smart enough, or deserving enough in order to receive the results we desire. The Right Questions don't care if we're good enough, smart enough, or deserving enough. They don't care what we think or what we feel.

The Right Questions enable us to look at the facts. Does this choice add to my life force? Will this bring me closer to my desired future? Is this an act of self-love? When we ask these questions before we make a choice and the answer is "No no no no" but we choose to do it anyway, at least we'll be clear that we are the ones who are sabotaging our future. Then, instead of being a victim of our circumstances, we can take ownership of them.

A moment of perfection comes when we give ourselves the gift of an empowering choice—a choice that is conscious, a choice that is consistent with our deepest desires. Each of us has the ability to create a lifetime of perfect moments simply by asking one or more of these questions. Then we can rightfully expect to arrive at the destination of our dreams.

3

Exposing Your Underlying Commitments

Our outer world reflects our inner commitments. If we want to know what we're really committed to, all we have to do is look at our lives. We are, whether we are aware of it or not, always creating exactly what we are most committed to. It is vital to understand that the choices we make are always in alignment with our deepest commitments. By examining what we have and what we don't have, we will be able to uncover and see what we are truly committed to. When our lives are not the way we want them to be, we can be certain that we have a conflicting hidden commitment to something other than that which we say we're committed to.

For example, you might declare that you are committed to financial security, but if you examine your choices carefully, you may discover that you spend more than you make every month. If you look deeper to see why you're not saving for the future or paying off your debts, you will undoubtedly uncover another commitment, a deeper one, which might be to spend your money where and when you want to. So when you see something you want, your natural response and your first commitment wins out. Without even thinking, you veer off course and obey your first commitment to spending your money instead of saving it.

Maybe you've made resolution after resolution to get in better physical shape, but when it's time to go work out you always have an excuse and wind up being too busy or too tired to keep your promise to yourself. It could be that when you look deeper you find that lying beneath the surface of this desire is a stronger commitment to feeling bad about yourself. Even though you wake up with the best intentions every day, when it comes to making smart choices about your health, your first commitment wins out and prevents you from taking an action that would lead you to achieving your goal.

It could be that you long to have a fulfilling sexual relationship with your spouse, but every time the opportunity arises you find a reason to avoid being intimate with him or her. Looking deeper, you might discover that even though you do have a genuine desire to have passionate sex with your spouse, there is another, deeper, commitment to punish him or her for not providing you with the things you desire. What better way to do this than to take yourself away when he or she longs to be near you? Again, your underlying commitment wins out.

Most of us don't even know that we have commitments other than the ones we're trying to manifest. That's why I call these hidden commitments *underlying* commitments: they exist at an unconscious level. They are our first commitments, and if they are not made conscious they will override any other desires. Our underlying commitments drive our thoughts, our beliefs, and—most important—our choices; they are the unseen forces that shape our realities. *Our underlying commitments are responsible for the discrepancy between what we say we want and what we're actually experiencing.*

These underlying commitments are formed by unconscious decisions we've made in the past. If you were raised by controlling parents, even though you think you long for discipline and structure, your life might always be in a state of chaos because your first commitment is to being a free spirit. Or it might be that you have an underlying commitment to stay safe, so your choices will be consistent with this commitment. Even when you long to ask for a promotion or take a leadership role, you won't be able to manifest your longing because your first commitment is to staying within the confines of your current reality. Or, in the dark recesses of your unconsciousness, you may have decided that you can't trust anyone and that it's easier to be alone. So even though you want love and intimacy in your life, you always choose the wrong mate because your first commitment is to being by yourself.

When you continually make choices that are in direct conflict with what you say you want, it is imperative that you expose their roots. When you find yourself baffled by the choices you make in the face of your stated intentions, check for underlying commitments. I promise you, they are there.

These underlying commitments keep us stuck in the same place year after year. Most of us just think of our unconscious choices as acts of weakness or bad luck, as familiar, known mistakes, errors, or misjudgments. We buy a new purse when we say we are committed to paying off our credit cards. We eat a cupcake when we say we are committed to losing weight. We deceive a loved one when we say we are committed to having an honest and intimate relationship.

Each time we set forth a new vision for ourselves, we are likely to come face-to-face with the underlying commitment that has controlled this area of our lives and prevented us from attaining this goal. I'll give you an example: My deepest desire at this time in my life is to be in the best physical health possible. This means that on my next birthday I will have more muscle mass, lower cholesterol, and richer blood and will be able to maintain forty minutes of intense aerobic exercise without panting like a tired dog. To achieve this goal, I will need to make healthy choices about everything I put in my body.

I want you to know that I already eat well. Any person examining my diet would tell me I was doing pretty well. But the other morning, after hearing from yet another doctor that I needed to look after my sugar intake and lower my cholesterol, what do you think the first thing I wanted to consume was? Well, I make this fantastic coffee drink. I take part of my son's chocolate protein shake and mix it with my coffee, and voilà—I have my morning fix. And this delicious drink just happens to be full of everything I am not supposed to have.

But on this particular morning, while going about this ritual in my automatic, trancelike state, I suddenly heard my inner voice say, "This drink is filled with caffeine and sugar. It isn't the wisest choice this morning given your health goal. What could you have instead?" I tried very hard to ignore this voice and even started arguing with it: "For God's sake, it's only one coffee drink" (my intellect); "Oh, but it makes me feel so cared for" (my emotions). But once I asked myself a Right Question—whether having this coffee drink was a choice of self-love or of self-sabotage—no matter how hard I tried, I couldn't hide the fact that I was about to make an unwise choice.

Clearly, I was about to begin my day with a choice that would disempower me rather than empower me. I was acutely aware that this choice would keep me stuck in a pattern from my past rather than taking me closer to my dream. In light of this realization, I had to question why I would be tempted to make this choice. I knew that I must have an unconscious first commitment to something other than my goal for attaining optimum health. I closed my eyes, took a deep breath, and asked myself, "What am I really committed to in this moment?"

What I heard was that I was more committed to receiving the comfort that this particular drink gives me. As I breathed in and listened to my inner wisdom, I could actually see an image of a part of me that was longing for some attention, comfort, and love.

Having brought my underlying commitment into my conscious awareness, I now could make one of two choices. I could ask myself how I could fill the needs of the part of me that wanted me to slow down and give it some attention. Several options came to mind—taking a walk by the beach, snuggling with my son, soaking in a warm bath. Or I could follow the orders of my first commitment and go for the quick fix. One choice would lead me in the direction of my deepest desire; the other choice would leave me further away.

This is the war, the internal struggle that goes on between our unconscious commitments and our soul's desires. Our soul longs for all the things that will bring us joy and fulfillment, while our unconscious, underlying commitments strive to be expressed and validated. Underlying commitments are so potent because they are our first commitments. Left unexamined, they will keep us stuck in the past and rob us of the future we deserve. Underlying commitments drive us to repeat the same self-sabotaging behaviors over and over again as they fuel our resignation. Since most of us were never taught about these underlying first commitments, we are unaware that they even exist. But uncover them we must, because as long as they remain hidden, our underlying commitments will continue to dictate our choices. We will be left to experience the stress and struggle that go along with saying we want one thing and doing another. We will continue to feel the powerlessness of not being able to attain the future we desire.

A DAY IN THE LIFE OF AN
UNDERLYING COMMITMENT

This is how it works: For the past four years you've been saying you want to lose twenty pounds, but here you are today not having met that objective. So you wake up and decide today is the day. You tell yourself, "I can do it! I'm going to make healthy choices." You begin the morning by eating a bowl of oatmeal and a slice of whole wheat bread and leave for work feeling empowered. Then, after eating a beautiful green salad for lunch, you have an urge for something sweet and decide to lean over and take a couple of bites of your best friend's cheesecake. It's so good that you just can't stop, and like any good friend you help her finish it off. Then, after a long day, you go for your favorite—a hamburger and fries—for dinner. You rationalize your choice by saying that you had time only to stop for fast food because you worked late and by God you deserve that burger anyway. For the moment you feel better. Guilt eludes you and your rationalization keeps you from looking around to see if there is a deeper cause for this choice. Your excuse for your inconsistent behavior stops you from unearthing the source of your self-sabotage. But then while you're getting ready for bed you begin to feel bad about the choices you made. The burger and fries no longer feel so good, and that moment of bliss turns on you quickly, becoming a source of shame, robbing you of your goals and desires and feeding your resignation. You go to sleep swearing that tomorrow will be a new day. You wake up wanting to eat well and stick to your diet, but sometime around 4 P.M., after having a healthy breakfast and lunch, you succumb once again to that urge for a little snack. Then you're off again and the cycle repeats itself. This is a day in the life of an underlying commitment.

Now, is this bad? It's bad only if you hate yourself for eating badly that day. It's a disempowering choice only if you beat yourself up when you get on the scale the next day and see that your weight hasn't moved in the direction you were hoping it would. It is horribly painful to make a commitment to an outward desire and then make choices that are in direct opposition to its fulfillment. Remember, this book is about getting where you want to go. It is not a book about losing weight. This is just an example of one of the most common human struggles. It is a clear example of saying you want one thing and having a first commitment that is opposing your heart's desire. When you are making choices that lead you away from your goal rather than closer to it, you know that you are operating on top of an underlying commitment.

If this example is familiar to you, I would ask you to become aware of what commitment is present for you when you are eating the cheesecake or other foods that are not supporting you in attaining your goal. You can do this by closing your eyes and asking yourself, "What am I committed to in this moment?" You might find that you are committed to using food to make you feel better, or to proving that you're too weak and can't do it on your own. Or maybe you'll discover that you are committed to eating whatever you want whenever you want it. This is very common: you don't like anyone telling you what to do, not even another part of yourself. So the internal struggle begins. One aspect of you would love to have a beautiful body or just to feel healthier, and another part of you can't stand being told what to do. You are at war, and the war is with yourself.

The only way to stop this inner battle is to first acknowledge that it is going on. You have to stop being a victim and realize that you have conflicting commitments. Only when you uncover the underlying commitment that is sabotaging your results will you begin to truly have choice. By asking the Right Questions and allowing yourself to hear the answers, you will automatically regain some power over your life. If you can consciously see that the choices you are making are an expression of your first commitment, you will set yourself free.

By exposing the underlying commitments that are driving your choices, you will be able to clearly see how you sabotage your success. You can be certain there is an underlying commitment directing your life when you engage in a series of disempowering choices that lead you away from your outward desire. Consider Helen's situation: Helen's goal was to pay off her debts and save enough money for a down payment on a house. For five years she dreamed that this would be the year that she would finally pay off her credit cards and begin saving money for her future. But year after year Helen found herself in the same financial condition she was in the year before. She always had an excuse for why she couldn't pay off her debts—unexpected medical bills, a new bike for her daughter, a trip back home to see her folks. She always had a reason to justify her financial situation. When I asked Helen about her debts, she was vague and unclear about how much money she owed and what a realistic plan to pay them off would look like. Helen had thought about seeking the guidance of a professional to help her create a plan to get her finances in order. But in the end Helen always made the choice to spend her time, money, and energy doing something else (choice number one).

When we looked further, we saw that any time Helen came into extra money, whether in bonuses or from extra work that she takes on, she did not send this money directly to the credit card companies. Instead, she chose to reward herself with something special for herself or her home (choice number two). Then we looked at her monthly expenses to see if there were ways in which she could lower her overhead in order to serve her long-term vision. Helen spent a good deal of her income on her fitness regime. In addition to her monthly gym membership fee, she paid for yoga classes, Pilates instruction, and martial arts training. Even though she spent much more on her fitness program than most people in her income range, she justified the expense, saying that with her full-time job and her responsibilities at home she needed to take extra good care of herself (choice number three).

Now, it's easy to justify Helen's behavior, saying that she works hard and deserves to spend her money on whatever she wants. But the fact remains that Helen is constantly stressed out because she spends more than she makes. She has had the same dreams and financial goals for over five years and has made only a little progress toward them. She blames others for her financial condition and uses her debt and lack of savings as a way to beat herself up and prove to herself that she is hopeless.

Ignoring our underlying commitments puts off the pain of dealing with our past choices but ensures that we will continue down the same path, away from our goals. It's imperative that we expose the commitments that have landed us in the situation that we find ourselves in. Helen is doing the same thing now that she did in the past. She is choosing to spend her money instead of saving for the future. Her first commitment is to having what she wants when she wants it, so she spends her money on whatever she deems important in the moment, without really looking at the long-term consequences of those short-term choices. Her magical thinking has her living in the hope that maybe someone, like her husband, will come through with the down payment for that house she desperately wants or that she will land a big job and magically be able to manage her money better than she is doing now. All of this leaves her going in familiar circles, hoping, wishing, and fantasizing that she will somehow miraculously land at her destination without having made new choices.

THE TRUTH WILL SET YOU FREE

The Right Questions are based on the simple idea that the truth will set you free. The truth releases us from the grip of our past. When we tell the truth, even if we don't like the fact that we have been committed to something other than what we say we've been striving for, we are liberated from our internal struggle. A beautiful Russian proverb states, "The bitter truth is better than a sweet lie." Our pain and suffering come from our perpetuating the lie by insisting, "But I'm committed to having an intimate relationship! I'm committed to being in great physical health! I'm committed to building my company and having a thriving career!" when we are in fact deeply committed to something else. Saying we want things without acknowledging our first commitments in these areas leaves us feeling powerless. But when we tell the truth—that what we're really committed to is something other than what we've been saying we are—our suffering subsides. Suffering is the result of our conflicting commitments.

We must expose our existing underlying commitments before we have the power to shift them. By exposing these unconscious commitments we gain the freedom to stand in the truth. Then we have the strength to be honest and say, "I've been wanting to create a successful career, but now I can see that my first commitment is to having someone else take care of me." Then, having acknowledged the truth, we can begin the process of transformation. Acknowledging our first commitment to having someone else take care of us will allow us to understand why we have consistently made choices that sabotage our success in our career. Then we will see that the choices we have made are in fact in perfect alignment with our first commitment. So in reality we have been creating exactly what we've been most committed to. When we expose the truth, we actually experience a profound shift in the way we feel about ourselves.

IDENTIFYING YOUR
UNDERLYING COMMITMENTS

Revealing the underlying commitments that prevent us from achieving our goals is the critical step that we need to take in order to turn our lives around. Each of us must have the courage to expose the lies we are telling ourselves. By making our first commitments conscious, we gain the ability to replace them with new, powerful commitments. Our intention in examining our first commitments is to expose them and embrace them. By bringing them into our full awareness and shedding light where there has been darkness, we are able to transcend our first commitments and create new, conscious commitments that are in alignment with our highest visions for the future.

To find your underlying commitments, write down a goal or desire that you've been unable to attain. Then make a list of all the actions you have taken or not taken in the past year that are in direct opposition to this goal. Now take your list and imagine that the choices that have taken you away from your desired goal or not brought you any closer to it are an expression of a deeper commitment, your first commitment. Next, close your eyes and ask yourself, "What commitment are these choices in direct alignment with?" There you will discover your underlying commitment.

It's important not to criticize ourselves for having these underlying commitments. They arose out of our need to compensate for things in our lives that either overburdened, overwhelmed, or undernourished us. We made these commitments at a time when we didn't have the freedom or the power to make our own outward choices. At some point in our lives, these first commitments served us. Now, having grown out of them, we can bring them into conscious awareness, acknowledge their use, and make new commitments and choices that will move us toward the future we desire.

The Right Questions expose the truth. When asked and answered, they reveal our deepest commitments, those that have been charting our negative choices. Until we begin asking these questions, our underlying commitments will continue to wreak havoc on our dreams. Once we bring these commitments out into the open, we will be able to examine them in light of our present-day awareness. It is only when we are present and aware that we can powerfully choose the direction of our lives.

We can't be traveling east and west at the same time. We are going either one way or the other. We can't lower our cholesterol while eating chocolate cake and fried chicken every day. We can't build a nest egg when we spend all our monthly income. We can't have an intimate relationship while deceiving our partner. It's unlikely that we will have the career of our dreams if we choose to stay in a job that feels safe and never take any risks. We won't meet our fitness objectives if we choose to sit in front of the TV instead of going out for our daily walk. We must choose our path.

If you really want to change your life, you must make new choices. The Right Questions wake you up and give you the power you need to change the direction of your life. Most important, they give you the inspiration to fulfill your deepest desires. Every time you make a new, empowering choice, every time you choose to turn your car around and head in the direction of your vision, you will be inspired by yourself and feel your flame roar. Each time you stop, slow down, and make a choice to nourish your soul, you will give yourself the confidence to fuel your journey to the destination of your dreams.

4

Will This Choice Propel Me Toward an Inspiring Future or Will It Keep Me Stuck in the Past?

Every choice we make leads us in one of two directions. We are headed either toward a future that inspires us or toward a past that limits us. When we're
moving in the direction of our deepest desires, we feel
the support of the entire universe behind us, and we are
inspired by our lives. Our excitement wakes us up in the
morning and gives us the motivation and energy we
need to forge ahead.

It doesn't matter what our vision is—whether it's to
make a million dollars, to spread love to the neighbor-
hood kids, to introduce a new law into action, or to become a teacher in middle school. When our actions
come straight out of our vision for our lives, we radiate

joy and our passion effortlessly carries us through our days.

Making choices that support our dreams gives us a tremendous sense of empowerment and self-esteem. When we see that we are making progress toward what we want out of our lives, we feel powerful, hopeful, and confident. Making choices that move us forward gives us the courage and the confidence to manifest our goals and desires.

On the other hand, choices made from fear keep us tied to the past. Our need for safety, security, and predictability prevents us from stepping outside the reality we know. Afraid of what we might find outside the comfort zone of what is familiar, we stay tied to the past, even when it no longer fulfills us. We are convinced that clinging to what we know will keep us safe, and we fear that leaving our past behind will put us in danger. In other words, the devil we know is better than the devil we don't know.

Our fear of expanding and taking risks causes us to believe that our dreams are unrealistic or out of reach. Our fears assert that we should be happy with what we've got. However, when we stop believing in ourselves, when we give up hope that we can be anything we want, a part of us begins to die. By depriving ourselves of our right to dream, to remember what we truly desire, we slowly lose our connection to our highest self. Often we feel that we've tried before and failed, so we're hesitant to try again. Our fear permeates our entire being, paralyzing us, keeping us from moving forward.

But here is the truth: you are either moving forward or you are moving backward. There is no middle ground. You are never stagnating, even if it appears that way at times. Every choice matters. Every choice, even though it might seem minor or inconsequential, is leading you in a particular direction. Even making the choice to do nothing at all will have an effect on your life. It's still a choice.

It's easy to see how the big choices shape our lives and our destinies. It's easy to deceive ourselves into believing that the small choices don't matter that much. But a hundred small choices in the wrong direction can add up to a lifetime where our dreams are always one step in front of us. If we can't fathom the consequence of not returning a phone call or paying our bills late, we just need to ask the first part of this Right Question: "Will this choice propel me toward an inspiring future?" If the answer is no, we must assume that our choice is leading us in the opposite direction.

Jim Rohn, the author of *Five Major Pieces to the Life*

Puzzle, says, "Failure is not a single cataclysmic event. We do not fail overnight. Failure is the inevitable result of an accumulation of poor thinking and poor choices. To put it more simply, failure is nothing more than a few errors in judgment repeated every day." So why are so many of us unaware of the choices we make each day that move us away from our goals rather than closer to them? Why do we continue repeating behaviors day after day that no long serve us? Because, as Rohn says, "the joy of the moment wins out to the consequences of the future." Since many of our behaviors go unrecognized, not only by ourselves but also by those around us, we assume they just don't matter. But they do. No action, no matter how small or seemingly inconsequential, goes unnoticed. Even if we think we're getting away with something, the universe knows the truth, and, deep down, so do we. We can go on for years fooling ourselves that we are headed in the direction of our dreams. But the state of our current affairs reflects the truth about our choices. In other words, the proof is in the pudding.

Marcus is a charming man in his late thirties who has built a successful career as a fitness trainer. Although

Marcus is great at what he does and enjoys his work, his deeper dream is to be an actor. Marcus is passionate about the arts and loves the way acting makes him feel. Committed to following his passion, Marcus attends acting classes and takes parts in local plays. He is a talented performer who always receives great reviews for his work. He says that he never feels as alive as he does when he's onstage. After years of seeing his acting as nothing more than a hobby, Marcus decided to slowly phase out of being a fitness trainer and devote himself to pursuing a full-time acting career.

But four years later, Marcus is further away from living his dream than ever. Despite his goal of becoming a professional actor, Marcus's actions and behaviors have clearly kept him stuck in the past, and have not moved him toward the future he longs for. I asked Marcus to make a list of all the daily choices he makes that lead him away from his goal. His list looked like this:

- I take on new clients all the time, leaving myself little time to pursue my acting career.

- I spend more than I earn every month, which makes it necessary to take on new clients to cover my overhead.

- I spend more time and energy developing my physical body than I do developing my craft.

- I listen to my internal dialogue, which tells me it's too hard and I am too old.

- I enroll in courses to develop my skills as a personal trainer instead of enrolling in acting classes to improve my performing skills.

Marcus justifies his choices by telling himself that he needs his fitness practice to fall back on in case his acting career doesn't work out. But having one foot in the boat and one foot onshore has kept Marcus's dreams on hold. With each day that passes he feels more momentum drawing him toward the past and away from the future.

Our minds are tricky. Most of us continue to fool ourselves day after day. The ability to rationalize behavior that goes against what we want in life might be our biggest curse, because it makes us masters at justifying our actions. By asking ourselves each day this Right Question—"Will this choice propel me toward an inspiring future or will it keep me stuck in the past?"—we get a fixed compass with which to monitor the direction of our lives. The moment we ask it, our eyes open. Then we can start to recognize how many of the choices that we make daily, weekly, and monthly are moving us toward our desired goals and how many send us sailing off course.

Bill had done very well for himself in his career as a senior corporate executive. By the age of fifty he had accomplished many of his professional goals and had acquired all the status, money, and accoutrements associated with success. But each morning as he pulled himself out of bed he became increasingly aware that there was something missing. Bill had no passion. Truth be told, it had been years since Bill had felt any enthusiasm about his job, but he stayed with it because it was what he knew and it felt safe. It may not have been what he wanted, but Bill decided it was better than the unknown. He went to work with the nagging awareness that he was doing nothing at all in this life that helped his fellow human beings. He ached inside to make a contribution.

Bill had long dreamed of working with an organization that was making a difference in the world. For years he had told himself that the time would come when he could pursue this dream. But deep inside Bill feared that if he followed his dream and failed he would be devastated. So he stayed where he was. Still, the conflict between his desire and his fears ate at him more with each passing day.

Bill began looking at his daily choices and asking himself, "Will this action propel me toward an inspiring future or will it keep me stuck in my past?" The jig was up. Bill could no longer postpone the moment of decision. Immediately, he began making choices that were more consistent with the future he desired.

Bill learned about a nonprofit organization whose sole mission was to transform people's lives. He was so inspired by the impact this organization was having on the world that he decided to volunteer his time and energy to serve its mission. He looked for every opportunity to contribute his talents and abilities. He wrote procedural manuals that improved the efficiency of the organization's events. Bill didn't hold back any of his passion or his energy. He immersed himself in the principles of the work itself and took it upon himself to learn all about the organization and its operations.

Bill began to feel a shift in his overall mood and energy. Although he was working more hours—at his regular job during the day and with this organization at night—he actually had more energy, and he felt more alive than he had in years.

In time Bill realized that this was the kind of work he had always longed to do. He initiated conversations with key people in the organization and wrote a proposal showing how his contribution could support its vision. Six months later Bill was offered the job of his dreams. Finally, Bill's desire to lead a more fulfilling life won out. By following his heart and giving up the familiarity of the past, Bill created a life for himself that he never dreamed possible. His work inspires him and fulfills his longtime yearning to make a difference in other people's lives. He begins each day with a sense of purpose and is energized and excited about his life.

Taking the risk to follow our hearts gives energy to our future and breathes life into our dreams. By stopping and asking ourselves if what we are doing is leading us toward an inspiring future or away from it, we gain the opportunity to remember our visions for our lives. Then we can honestly see how many of our choices are leading us in the right direction and how many are leading us astray.

This question can alter your life in an instant—because as soon as you realize you're headed in the wrong direction, you have the power to make a new choice, a choice that can deliver you the life you desire.

5

Will This Choice Bring Me Long-Term Fulfillment or Will It Bring Me Short-Term Gratification?

Most of us long to create a future that is fulfilling and inspiring. We spend countless hours dreaming about the day when our goals will be satisfied and our hearts content. This question—"Will this choice bring me long-term fulfillment or will it bring me short-term gratification?"—is vital for all of us who are committed to making our dreams into realities. Staying focused on our long-term desires is essential as we go about our day-to-day activities, because it's so easy to get sidetracked and experience a momentary lapse in memory just as we're about to move powerfully toward our desired futures. When we ask this question before we make a choice, we are able to tell if we are choosing to stay on the path of our dreams or take a detour from our desired destination.

To have long-term fulfillment, we must stand in the vision for our future. It takes a certain amount of tenacity and focus to stay on course. It's human nature to opt for the quick fix, preferring to suffer the consequences of our behavior . . . later. Our desires in the moment win out over our commitments for the future.

Choices made in the heat of the moment, without a thought for their consequences, are choices based on instant gratification. They come unannounced, usually in the form of a compulsion, an impulse, or a craving. They can sneak up on us unexpectedly and are otherwise known by their alias, the "dream-robbers." When we make choices responding to an urge, an impulse, or a whim, we can be certain that they are based on instant gratification rather than long-term fulfillment.

Instant gratification is often an illusion. It is an attempt to fool ourselves. The truth is that it isn't really gratifying to make a choice that interferes with our future plans. My brother Michael told me, "'Instant gratification' is a misnomer because it's not a fair assessment of what's really going on. It should be called 'instantaneous gratification,' because it's over as soon as it's finished.

You're attempting to gratify yourself quickly, but remorse sets in as soon as you realize that you are left further away from your goal. The rush is over, but the guilt stays with you."

The reality is that choices that support our long-term fulfillment aren't always fun. They aren't the easiest or the sexiest choices to make. But making choices with our future in mind is vital if we want to make our vision for our lives a reality.

When we make choices that are in direct conflict with our dreams, we rob ourselves of the future we desire. Fooling ourselves that we will arrive at our destination as we veer off our route is a mean joke. Instant gratification ensures that we will travel in the same vicious circles again and again. As the psychologist Rollo May once said, "Insanity is doing the same things over and over again and expecting different results." If we want a new future that does not look like our past, we must make new choices in the present. We are masters at rationalizing and kidding ourselves, tricking ourselves into believing that things will magically get better. But remember, the small choices that are in direct alignment with our long-term vision are the doorway to the future we desire.

Most of us, at some time in our lives, have been driven to make impulsive decisions that have led us off the path of our dreams and down a long, dark road to nowhere. Maybe you remember a time when you had an uncontrollable craving for a hot fudge sundae just after you'd begun your diet. Or maybe you've been caught catalogue shopping after having finally paid off that high-interest credit card. These yearnings come quickly and, when left unattended, will cause us to forget what we are committed to, only to fill a need in that moment.

Denise has been divorced for more than twenty years and is a few months shy of her fiftieth birthday. She came to me desperately wanting to figure out why she had not met the man of her dreams. Her desire to fall in love and get remarried had been haunting her for years. Denise's long-standing story about why she doesn't have the relationship she desires was that she never meets the right kind of men. This was as good an excuse as any for why she was still single after all these years. But on closer look we discovered a deeper truth: Denise goes out only with men who are ten to fifteen years younger than she—men who are looking for some short-term fun, not a long-term, committed partnership. So instead of staying true to her deepest desire and looking to meet someone who wants the same things she does, Denise opts for the quick fix of a night of fun. The fun usually only lasts a few weeks and then she is left feeling alone, no closer to her goal than she was a few weeks before.

Why do we opt for quick fixes, preferring to suffer the consequences later? When we consistently go off the path to our dreams, we can be certain that there is an unconscious need that is trying to get our attention. Since most of us don't take the time to care for our inner world, the only way our unconscious needs can be met is by our acting them out through our impulses and urges.

If you're human, you most likely have many unfulfilled needs that you are either aware of or not. These needs are always lurking in the background, looking for opportunities to be taken care of. If we do not make the conscious choice to fulfill these underlying needs, they become intruders, grabbing for whatever short-term fix will satisfy them in the moment.

Often we use the same behavior to fulfill different unconscious needs. One day you might eat chocolate cake because you're feeling depressed. The next day you eat it because you're angry with your wife, and the next day because you're feeling unfulfilled at work. We act on these impulses because we're trying to change the way we feel and the quick fix offers us the hope of finding some comfort for ourselves now. We try to medicate ourselves by doing something that is ultimately not good for us. But what looks like comfort in the moment is in reality a form of self-punishment.

It is vital that we recognize and tend to our unmet needs, because if we don't take the time to care for them we will constantly find ourselves headed down paths that lead us away from our goals rather than toward what we desire. When we don't deal with the unfulfilled needs inside us, they continue to drive us to act impulsively, to forsake our long-term vision in favor of short-term gratification. Then our unfulfilled needs, not our vision, drive our behaviors.

Bob, forty years old and a trader on Wall Street, avoids dealing with his feelings at all costs. Once very wealthy, he's been struggling with his personal finances for the past six years. Bob refuses to deal with the reality of his financial situation and thus is able to avoid feeling the pain of his past mistakes and his financial losses. If he allowed himself to really feel all the devastation, and his shame over what he has done with his money, he would be able to give his situation a proper assessment and make a new plan. But instead he makes the situation worse by acting on the same impulses that drove him to the financially vulnerable situation he finds himself in today. I shared with Bob my friend Dennis Schmucker's Theory of the Hole, which says, "When you're in one, stop digging."

Finally, when Bob was completely beaten down by his failed attempts to regain control, he was confronted with the fact that all his efforts to gain his money back were quick fixes that ended up worsening his situation and severely raising his anxiety level. When Bob was forced to face the reality of his situation, he was overcome with the feelings of shame and devastation that he had long avoided. By dealing with those feelings rather than trying to camouflage them with one more get-rich-quick scheme, Bob was able to ask the Right Questions and take the actions that he knew would lead him to long-term financial stability.

There is a brand of delusion that has us believe that we will find the way out by digging further in. We go on a shopping spree because we kept to our budget for a month. We continue to gamble when we've just lost a month's wages. We work out at the gym for two hours and reward ourselves with a vanilla shake.

There is a paradox in all this, because even though we need to stay focused on our long-range plans, at the same time we don't want to deprive ourselves of enjoyment in our day-to-day lives. The important distinction is that not all choices that involve instant gratification are bad. Some people are so future-focused that they deprive themselves of having any fun. We all need to let down our guard at times and just go for some momentary pleasure. We all deserve the right to indulge from time to time; we just need to be mindful not to indulge in the areas of our lives where we are struggling. So if your primary goal is to lose weight, you need to be conscious when thinking about indulging your desires in this area. Likewise, if your goal is to save money, indulging a craving to eat a hot fudge sundae might be a better choice for you than giving in to the urge to buy a $300 jacket.

The questions you must ask yourself are "Will taking this action rob me of the future I desire?" and "Do I really have choice in this area of my life, or am I acting on an unconscious need?" This Right Question—"Will this choice bring me long-term fulfillment or will it bring me short-term gratification?"—should be used when you aren't getting any closer to your desires, when the same goals remain unattained year after year, and when you find yourself repeating the same behaviors time and again.

This question can be an important guide for you to follow as you go about your day. It will support you in examining and dissecting the automatic behaviors you catch yourself in. Only when you stand in the highest vision of your life will you be able to see if your choices will ultimately serve your long-range vision. Using this question allows you to give up something you want for something you want more. It will provide a firm barometer for you to use in determining whether the choices you make today will serve you in the future.

6

Am I Standing in My Power or Am I Trying to Please Another?

This powerful question—"Am I standing in my power or am I trying to please another?"—challenges us to believe in ourselves and make the daring choice to trust in our innate ability to know what's in our highest and best interest. Standing in our power requires us to let go of the need to make others like us and instead stand committed to honoring ourselves, even if our choices go against popular opinion. To stand in our power we must be bold and confident and have the courage to stand up for ourselves. Standing in our power demands that we be vulnerable, listen to our own voice, and take risks outside the comfort of what we know. Claiming all of our power requires us to throw the dice, take our best shot, and go for our best life.

None of us really knows if what we think, what we want, or what we believe will bring us the future we desire. Too often, we think others know better. It's so easy to minimize our abilities, claiming, "I'm not sure" or "I don't know how" or "They know more than me." But none of these declarations will provide us with any peace or any power. Often we let our fears of not being strong enough, smart enough, or deserving enough win out. Owning our power means honoring the fact that each of us was put on this earth with everything we need to live a life full of purpose and meaning. Owning our power means claiming the credibility and uniqueness of our own humanity. It means trusting in our own brilliance to guide us. Standing in our power calls on us to discover and then to declare what's right and what's not right for us. When we stand grounded in our personal truth and take charge of our lives, we take the courageous leap of faith that is needed to transcend our fears and walk through the intimidation of others.

It doesn't matter who we are—how rich, famous, talented, or educated. At some point each of us will face the choice of claiming our power or giving it away by trying to please someone else. A few nights ago I had a chat with my friend Alanis Morissette, the brilliant poet and seven-time Grammy winner, about the importance of standing in our power and fighting for what we believe is right, even when it goes against popular opinion. Both of us had too many examples of times early in our careers when we relinquished our power to someone we believed knew more than we did. She shared with me an experience she'd had several years earlier, after the tremendous success of her debut album, *Jagged Little Pill*. Alanis was committed to delivering her message in a particular way and had a strong desire to write and direct her own music video. But her desire was met with strong opposition. Music industry executives tried their best to dissuade her, telling her that directing her own video wasn't the smart thing to do and that she was too inexperienced and therefore incapable of overseeing the project. They even went so far as to say that by making the video she would single-handedly ruin her career. Many of the people closest to her also reacted to the idea with fear and mistrust. Although Alanis felt sad, frustrated, and disappointed by the lack of support from those she trusted, she made the choice to move forward anyway, valuing her instincts as an artist more than any desire of hers to please or meet the expectations of those around her.

Alanis stood in her power and claimed her right to deliver her music in a way that was true to her personal integrity. She nurtured herself through her creative endeavor and in the end wound up loving not only the result but the entire process. Alanis told me, "I know that each experience of standing in my power feeds the one that follows. Standing up for myself helped me build my confidence to be at the helm, to direct, and eventually to produce my own music. I would never be where I am now if I had listened to those who wanted me to relinquish my power or if I had deferred to others to creatively define me."

Alanis had the courage to take her power and make her dream a reality. Even though the ride was rough, she persevered, trusting that no matter where she landed it would be the perfect place for her. She gave herself the gift of being true to her own personal integrity.

In order to create the life of our dreams, we need a strong foundation on which to build who we are and what we stand for. We build this unshakable foundation by living within the structure of our own personal integrity. When we are in our power, we are deeply rooted in our truth, which means we honor our needs, our desires, and ourselves. When we are living a life of integrity, we follow the guidelines that are in direct alignment with our soul's desires. When we are aligned with our highest selves, we trust ourselves enough to follow our hearts. Then we are able to be straight and tell the truth about who we are and what we want, even if it disappoints someone else.

On the other hand, we know when we are wavering and disconnected from our integrity, because at those times we feel timid and intimidated. We give up our needs and desires in order to gain the love of others. Every time you try to please another and forsake your own truth for theirs, you relinquish some of your power. You forget who you are and hand to others the reins of your life. Each and every day you have the opportunity to claim the right to stand up for yourself or to give your power away. Claiming our power requires us to stand for the greatest expression of ourselves while honoring the highest and most sacred aspects of our humanity.

Owning our power requires us to accept ourselves as we are. It means accepting our strengths and weaknesses, our brilliance and our flaws, no matter what anyone else may think about us. When we are living lives infused with integrity, we feel strong enough to be true to our own desires.

Any time we are living outside of our personal integrity, we put up barriers that prevent us from translating our dreams into reality. In any area of our lives where we fail to act from integrity or violate our own understanding of what is right or wrong for us, we fall prey to putting the outside world's needs before our own. We then disconnect from the enormity of our power and our ability to create what we want.

When we are not being true to our personal integrity, we cut ourselves off from our innate intelligence and can no longer hear the voice of our own inner wisdom. Our inner wisdom speaks to us through our instincts. When we don't trust our instincts, we place all our power outside ourselves.

I had this experience myself recently, when my instincts gave me repeated warning signs that something wasn't right and I continued to ignore these internal signals. In December of last year I purchased the house of my dreams. Situated on a hill overlooking the Pacific, the house had everything I wanted, including breathtaking panoramic views. Its only flaw was that the house was a bit too small for my son and me. I am someone who loves to remodel houses, though, so I set out on the task of finding an architect who could support me in making this house my perfect palace. After interviewing two people for the job, I chose the one who told me every-thing I wanted to hear—that I could have the design I wanted and have the work completed within my budget and within six months.

But that didn't happen. After three months had gone by and none of the work had been delivered on sched-ule, I began to feel suspicious and increasingly con-cerned. I met with my architect weekly, hoping that he would say something to ease my growing anxiety. Al-though he never gave me direct answers to my ques-tions, he smiled a lot and said things like, "Don't worry about it. Everything is under control. I know what I'm doing." I came away from our weekly meetings feeling a little better but never quite silencing the increasingly nagging inner voice that told me things were not at all okay and that I wasn't standing up for myself.

Normally, I am a person who claims a great deal of my power. Under any other circumstance—with an em-ployee, with my agent, with a publisher, or with friends—I would never be satisfied with vague answers. But because I told myself that this person was the expert, that he knew more than I did, and because he was a personal friend on top of it, I talked myself out of taking a stand on my own behalf. I ignored my inner voice and put my head in the sand, trying to pretend that everything was okay. In retrospect I can see all the things I didn't do that ended up costing me my power in this situation. Here are a few of them:

- I never had my attorney read over the contract.

- I didn't trust my instincts to get an outside opinion when key promises hadn't been kept.

- Because my architect was a personal friend, I never bothered to check his references.

- I never confronted the fact that I had lost my trust in him—either to him or to myself.

Of course, I had many other options available to me. I could have asked my architect to stop all work until my concerns were addressed. I could have called in another architect to check his work and tell me exactly what was going on. But my fear of having a confrontation with the man I hired and having him *not like me* kept me silent and ended up costing me more money than I care to admit and a year and half of time. Mine was a costly mistake; yours doesn't have to be.

I share this experience to illustrate how easy it can be to turn over our power to another person or situation, and how tempting it sometimes is to ignore our inner voice. Our instincts are like a barometer; they let us know when we have assigned our power to someone else. Our instincts whisper in our ears, "Wake up and pay attention. Something's wrong. They shouldn't be treating me like this." Our instincts are the proverbial knock on the door, saying, "Hey in there, something isn't right! Don't do it!" If we shrink at the thought of confrontation, chances are we will feel too intimidated to speak our truth. We may tell ourselves that others know more, that they are smarter or have more experience and therefore their authority should not be questioned. But when we deny our natural instincts and put others' happiness before our own, we turn away from our truth and hand over our power on a silver platter.

In order to stand fully in our power we have to become comfortable with confrontation. We have to give ourselves permission to rock the boat and make some waves. We must trust that it is more important that we stick up for ourselves than that we gain the approval of others.

Pleasing others is a habit that some of us developed when we were young. We learned that if we did something special—if we were cute, danced, used good manners, or received good grades in school—we would gain the affection and the approval we desired. Some of us learned that we had to forsake our own needs to fit in with our families. We kept our opinions to ourselves. We stayed silent, even when we longed to share our views. We followed along with the crowd rather than making waves. For most of us, this pattern of behavior began in our interactions with our parents. Now this habit is embedded deep in our psyches. We've learned to give away our power for the approval of others. We deny ourselves the gift of our voice, our opinions, and our authentic expression. Obligations, "should"s, and guilt become the dictators of our actions.

When we're stuck in the pattern of people-pleasing, we do not have access to making clear choices. We are driven to fulfill others' needs in order to be loved. In order to stand in our power we must have the option of just saying *no*. We have to be willing to give up the need for others' approval and give up our need to make others happy. The truth is that not everyone will like us and it's not our job to make others happy—just as it isn't the job of others to make us happy.

It's so easy to give our power away to oblige our partners or console our families. But if the choices we make
rob us of too much of our private time, if they deprive us
of our joy or our inner peace or prevent us from expressing our creative gifts, then ultimately they are violations
we are perpetrating against our own souls. These violations do not affect just us in negative ways; they affect
all those around us. When we don't take care of ourselves
because we are trying to make others happy, we build up
resentment toward the very people we are trying to please.
Recently, my friend Jen had this experience while taking
some time off for herself.

After working for twenty-one days without a break,
Jen was feeling depleted and undernourished. She un-
abashedly declared to her family, co-workers, and friends
that she was taking some time to nourish her soul and
get the rest she needed. She and her boyfriend, Jeff, set
out to spend a night at a local hotel and spa for some
rest and relaxation. Jen woke up the next morning with
the delicious reality of having nothing on the agenda.
The whole day stretched out before her and she was free
to do whatever she pleased. Then Jeff innocently asked
if they could have breakfast with one of his friends. Jen's

first internal reaction was "Absolutely not. This is *my* day." She had wanted to go to the gym before her afternoon massage, and going to breakfast with Jeff's friend would make this impossible.

Even though Jen had really wanted time to be alone, she decided that the "nice" thing to do was to say yes and go to breakfast. She rationalized this choice by telling herself that Jeff's friend was in town for only a couple of weeks and that this might be the only opportunity she would have to meet him. She went on to justify her choice by thinking of how she would never want anyone to deny her the right to see one of her out-of-town friends, so how could she deny Jeff's request? She told herself, "What harm will one hour spent at breakfast cause? In the grand scheme of things, this choice really doesn't matter."

But within minutes of saying yes, Jen became angry and regretful that she had so easily given up her precious alone time in an attempt to please her partner. In doing so, she had ignored her deep need to have her weekend be all about her. She fell into the familiar pattern of putting others' needs before her own. By the time breakfast was over Jen was feeling powerless and deeply rooted in her resentment. And as is so often the case, she was mad not only at herself but also at Jeff for not intuitively being aware of her needs. Jen even deprived herself of receiving the full benefit and enjoyment of her afternoon massage because she was so busy reprimanding herself and feeling disappointed that she had let herself down.

Then, as she was lying by the pool later in the day, Jen remembered the Right Questions. The question that immediately came to her mind was "Am I standing in my power or am I trying to please another?" She closed her eyes and looked back in time to see whether, had she asked herself this question before she said yes to Jeff's request, she would have been able to see where this choice would lead her. She remembered the morning and how they had awakened with nowhere to be and nothing to do. She remembered her commitment to having a weekend of complete relaxation and doing only those things that would restore her balance and well-being. She then thought about Jeff's request and asked herself, "Would getting dressed and going to breakfast nourish me, or would I be doing it to please someone else?" When she put it in those terms, Jen could clearly see that making this choice was in fact a violation of her own needs and now understood why she was left feeling even more depleted than before. By making the choice to not be true to herself, Jen relinquished her power to care for herself. If Jen had just taken thirty seconds to ask herself this Right Question, she could have stayed true to herself and changed the whole direction of her precious weekend off.

Why couldn't Jen see this before she went through hours of pain and process? It's really quite simple. Jen's first commitment is to be "nice": to take care of others and to *not* be selfish. In her mind, choosing what's best for her is selfish, so she automatically chooses to put others' needs first. Some of you might be thinking she made the right choice—that the needs of her boyfriend should come before her own. But any time we forsake our own needs for the needs of another, we ultimately damage our relationship with that person.

This Right Question allows us to stand in our power and be clear about our priorities. If I choose to ignore myself when I am in desperate need of my own attention, I will resent those I have deemed more important than me. Even though I might spend the day trying to be happy and pleasant, underneath I will feel angry because I have made a choice that depleted me. This underlying resentment will inevitably come out no matter how hard I try to deny what I feel.

We set ourselves up to lose every time we give away our power and minimize the importance of our own needs. Many people I work with truly believe that they don't matter. They think it's okay to abandon themselves as long as they are making someone else happy. They tell themselves that they are strong enough to withstand the neglect as long as it's in the name of making someone else happy. Or they tell themselves that it's their job to be the sacrificial lamb. This is often what we were taught when we were young, and it sets us up to violate ourselves and play the part of the martyr. Each time we ignore our own needs to please another, we disconnect from our own ability to love and nurture ourselves. Please remember that pleasing another is not the same as caring for another. The important thing to realize is that we can't really care for another if we do not first care for ourselves. By consulting ourselves to see whether the choices we make come from a place of standing in our power or one of needing to please another, we are forced to confront the subtle and not so subtle ways in which we violate ourselves.

This Right Question will support you in reclaiming your power in every aspect of your life. You may feel that you have your power in some areas of your life, but certain people and situations are bound to come along that will temporarily blindside you. It is precisely at those moments that I invite you to remember to breathe deeply, check in with yourself, and ask yourself this important question.

7

Am I Looking for What's Right or Am I Looking for What's Wrong?

The question "Am I looking for what's right or am I looking for what's wrong?" has the power to shift a moment of despair into a moment of delight. When we look for what's right, we consciously refocus the lens of our perceptions. Suddenly we are able to see the good in every situation and every person. For most of us, looking for what's right is not our natural way of viewing the world. In fact, most of us are trained to scan for what's wrong in any given relationship or situation. But when we make the choice to look for what's right, a whole new reality emerges.

People who are successful in life look for what's right. Let me give you an example. There are more than seven hundred Realtors in the seaside village of La Jolla, California, where I live, and probably less than twenty who do most of the business. I had the privilege of working with one of these twenty, a man by the name of Ozstar Dejourday. Every time I reached Ozstar's voice mail, I was greeted by his upbeat voice: "Thank you for calling. Wow, what a great life we have living in beautiful La Jolla, California!" Just hearing this message inspired me to stand up tall, put a smile on my face, and breathe in with gratitude. Ozstar is a man who looks for what's right.

One day I asked Ozstar to share with me what inspires him to bring his infectious positive attitude to everyone he meets. I wanted to discover what powerful lens he looks through that causes him to see life as such a magical parade. He looked at me, and with a big grin on his face he said, "Your eyes, your mind, and your heart were given to you for free and so was the air, the water, and the sunlight. How could you not be grateful for all these precious gifts! That's why the words *thank you* are the most important ones in any language. When we say, 'Thank you,' we are present to all our gifts and the love that we share." Ozstar's refreshing perspective reminded me of one of my favorite quotes, by Marcel

Proust: "The real voyage of discovery consists not in seeking new landscapes, but in having new eyes."

When we are looking for what's right, we invite life to shower us with all its many gifts. Looking for what's right opens our hearts and allows us to live in a state of gratitude for what we have. It lets us appreciate the little things that bless us every day. It causes us to stop taking for granted the many gifts in our lives. Just think of all the things we have to be grateful for! The fact that you are reading this book means that you have the ability to read, as well as the resources to buy a book or access to a library. Your heart is pumping, your lungs are breathing, and you have the priceless ability to see, feel, taste, and smell. These are extraordinary gifts! The state of gratitude lives within each of us, and when we stop and ask this question, we gain immediate access to the level of consciousness where love and gratitude reside. When we look for what's right, we inspire our children, our friends, our co-workers, and our communities.

Looking for what's right is an art that takes practice. But here is the payoff: when we look for what's right, we feel good, strong, and worthy. When we look for what's wrong, we feel bad, resigned, and disappointed.

It's easy to look for what's wrong. For most of us, this

is our default way of viewing the world. We are experts at describing in great detail what isn't right about our jobs, our mothers, our relationships, our teachers, our children, our bodies, our government, and our bank accounts. When we look for what's wrong, we choose to view our lives through the narrowest possible lens, zooming in on the places where our expectations haven't been met, where others have failed to meet our needs, where the world doesn't look the way we have decided it should. When we're looking for what's wrong, our eyes focus on the negative qualities of others, spotting their weaknesses and their incompetencies.

In addition to immediately shifting our perspective and thus our mood, what this question does is show us that maybe—just maybe—what's wrong is not "over there" with others. Maybe the problem lives not outside us but rather in our own lenses, the ones through which we choose to view the world. We can easily argue against this point and say that our spouses *are* wrong, that our bosses *are* wrong, and that the waitress who brought the wrong kind of salad dressing is wrong, too. But what we can be assured of is that if we look for what's wrong in any given situation, we will find it. And then our experience will be one of disappointment and discontent.

The moment we find something wrong, we automatically point our fingers in blame at the other person or the situation. It's so easy to find fault. Finding fault with others is the lazy person's out. I've done it a million times myself. I've pointed my finger at others instead of taking responsibility for the reality I see. I have been guilty of blaming my boss, my boyfriend, my coach, and even my mother for my discontent. Making others wrong becomes an excuse we use to justify our moods and bad behavior. By focusing on what's wrong, we avoid taking responsibility.

Last month, I asked a group of ten people to dwell on this question and to notice how many times each day they make themselves, another person, or a particular event in their lives wrong. Here is what they reported:

Naomi received an e-mail from a friend that contained a picture of her. As Naomi looked at the picture, her first thought was, "Oh my God, I really look like hell." All she could see were her flaws—the crookedness of her teeth, the wrinkles near her eyes, the loose skin on her neck. Everything about the picture was wrong. Naomi even went so far as to make the photographer wrong for not getting her at a better angle!

When she realized that she had been focused entirely on what was wrong with her, Naomi decided to spend the same amount of time looking for what was right. She made a list of all the things about her body that she was grateful for, and all the things she could find in herself that were right. She was grateful that she is amazingly healthy, that she has a strong body and a warm heart. She felt grateful that she smiles often and that she has loving, sparkling eyes. She appreciated her tanned skin and her beautiful blond hair. Naomi's mood lifted instantly when she started looking for what was right.

Kim saw how she made things wrong in seemingly little ways. One night she was enjoying an interesting conversation with her husband when she began to notice him taking sip after sip of his juice. She became so engrossed in her judgments about how often he took sips of his juice that she could barely concentrate on what had been a great conversation. Instead of looking at what was right about him she was focused on the one thing that annoyed her in that moment. Kim suddenly realized that by focusing on what was wrong she was making the choice to deprive herself and her husband of sharing an intimate evening together.

Kim caught herself, took a deep breath, and looked into her husband's eyes. There she was reminded of everything that she loves about this man and was awakened to the countless gifts he brings into her life every day. Asking this question allowed Kim to transform a moment of pettiness and frustration into a moment of sincere love and gratitude.

Erin had waited six years to get pregnant and begin the family she'd always wanted. When she gave birth to Jonathan, she was convinced that he was the most perfect creature on the planet. Now five years old, Jonathan attends kindergarten. When Erin arrived at Jonathan's school one day, his teacher made an offhand remark about Jonathan's habit of picking his nose. Erin was horrified. She knew Jonathan occasionally displayed this unattractive behavior at home, but she felt embarrassed and ashamed that he was now doing it at school. As she grew more preoccupied with her son's bad habit, Erin seemed to lose sight of the bigger picture—that she was blessed with a healthy, funny, creative, and loving child. The more Erin reprimanded Jonathan for his actions, the more he acted out, sometimes picking his nose right in front of her just to gain her attention.

Finally, when Erin realized she was just focusing on what was wrong with her son, she decided to give up trying to fix his behavior and instead focus her attention on all the things that were right about Jonathan. At bedtime after she read him his good-night story, Erin began stroking his head and telling him all the things she loved about him. Within a few days Jonathan had stopped acting out and instead seemed to be thriving in the presence of his mother's approval.

It was one of the busiest weeks of the year for Ed, who works as the production manager for a trade show company. He was in the midst of handling a thousand details before a big show when he received a phone call from his boss asking him to please drop what he was doing and come to the corporate office for a short meeting. On the way to the meeting Ed became aware that his mood had drastically changed. Earlier in the day he had been happily working, but now he was feeling antsy and angry. In a moment of awareness Ed asked himself, "Right now, am I looking for what's right or am I looking for what's wrong?" Ed soon understood why his mood had so radically shifted. Not only was he making the meeting wrong; he was making his boss wrong for asking him to be there and making himself wrong for not wanting to go. He called me and said, "Okay, Debbie, I get it. I see what I'm doing and it's making me miserable. And as of this moment I am going to choose to make the whole situation right."

Ed took a deep breath and made a new choice, declaring that it was absolutely perfect that he was going to a meeting in the middle of the day. He thought of all the things he could appreciate about the unexpected change in plans: it gave him a chance to get out of the office for a little while and to connect with his co-workers before the upcoming show. By simply switching his perspective from wrong to right Ed was able to slip back into a state of contentment and give himself permission to relax and enjoy himself during the meeting.

This might be the most important question we can ask ourselves if we are truly committed to living a life filled with ease and contentment. Abraham Lincoln reminds us that we are only as happy as we make up our minds to be. Looking for what's wrong prevents us from seeing the perfection that exists in our lives right now. We must all ask ourselves what would happen if we changed the lens through which we view the world. How would our lives alter if we saw our co-workers as divine beings who are here to impart essential wisdom to us? What would happen if we listened to our neighbors as though they were the wisest people in the world? Would they show up any differently than they do right now? What would be possible if we approached our partners as though their sole purpose was to bring us ecstasy and joy? What would we hear? What would we see? What would be possible? Looking for what's right is a life-enhancing choice—a choice that promises peace, contentment, and fulfillment.

8

Will This Choice Add to My Life Force or Will It Rob Me of My Energy?

Our life force is the key to our survival. Without it, we cease to exist. Our life force, which the Chinese call *chi*, the Japanese call *ki*, and Ayurveda calls *prana*, has been described as the vital energy that breathes life into our bodies. Our life force is the guardian of our minds, our bodies, and our souls. Asking this Right Question—"Will this choice add to my life force or will it rob me of my energy?"—allows us to see whether the choice we are about to make will strengthen our life force and support us in keeping our inner flame roaring, strong, and vibrant or will rob us of our vital energy. We each have a choice, and with each action we either feed or starve our life force. This question immediately reminds us that every choice, decision, and action we take has an impact on our deepest selves and our sense of well-being.

Most us take our life force for granted. We unconsciously go about our lives thinking that we are immortal, taking our health for granted and ignoring the needs of our bodies. But in the moments when we are fully awake, we can't help but feel and appreciate the great gift that has been bestowed on us—the gift of being alive. If each of us were present to how precious our life force is, we would care for it as we would a newborn child. We would live in awe of the miracle of our existence. When we are awake to the preciousness of life, we go though our days respecting the fact that our life force needs feeding and nourishment. We automatically ask ourselves how we can take care of and protect this precious energy.

Each day we are faced with a multitude of choices. We decide what we will eat, how much rest and exercise we will give our bodies, and at what pace we will go about our daily activities. Each choice we make either adds to our life force or robs us of our vitality. In essence we are either growing or dying, expanding or contracting. Every time we make a choice to nurture our life force, we choose life. Each time we choose actions that drain us of our energy, we are weakening our internal flame.

It's so easy to forget that our bodies are a delicate gift—a temporary home for our souls. It's usually only in times of great pain—such as when we are faced with the death of a loved one or a serious illness—that we are aware of the impermanence of life. In those moments when we come face-to-face with our own mortality or that of our loved ones, we become profoundly aware of how important it is to make choices that strengthen, rather than deplete, our life force.

When our life force is threatened, we desperately look to the outer world to regain our lost vitality. Anne is a good example of this. Anne had spent the past seventeen years running around aimlessly trying to get her life together. Plagued by intense loneliness, she went from husband to husband and boyfriend to boyfriend, only to wind up at age fifty without a mate. For years she smoked marijuana and cigarettes in an attempt to numb her deep emotional pain. Over the years, whenever I met with Anne, I sensed this pain. Anne knew that not only was she a disappointment to herself but she was setting a horrible example for her two now grown children, whom she loved dearly.

Anne's deepest desire was to be a great mom and to have her children respect her. But she had failed miserably at her goal. When the pain became too great for her to bear, Anne finally committed to looking at her life with clear eyes. She knew there was no way she could be a nourishing influence on her children if she continued making choices that diminished her vitality. Anne made a list of all the behaviors she had been engaging in that were robbing her of her life force. Her list looked like this:

- I wake up late in the morning.

- I go from job to job, never sticking with anything.

- I smoke pot regularly.

- I smoke cigarettes.

- I hide my behavior from my children.

- I procrastinate paying my bills.

- I show up late.

- I don't keep up with my personal commitments.

- I try to pretend I have it together when I don't.

- I flake out on my children.

- I constantly reprimand myself for all of my bad behaviors.

It was easy for Anne, in reading over her list, to see that she was draining herself of her life force and that a part of her was dying every day because she was choosing behaviors and taking actions that were really self-destructive. She had known this for some time but had not been able to change her behavior. When she saw the items on her list simply as those things that didn't enhance her life force, and not as proof of how worthless she was, her perspective began to shift.

Examining the list, Anne started thinking, "If this is what drains me of my energy and thus my ability to change, what would create the opposite?" With a lot of courage and some help from friends, Anne made a new list—of choices that would strengthen her life force. Making the commitment to live her life in a way that was consistent with her vision of being an extraordinary mother, and grandmother, she came up with a list of choices that supported her newfound resolve:

- Stop smoking.

- Go to Narcotics Anonymous meetings.

- Hire a life coach.

- Eat foods that nourish my well-being.

- Read daily meditations.

- Move closer to my children.

- Listen with genuine interest to my children's needs and respond accordingly.

- Spend quality time with my grandson.

In less than six months Anne's world began to shift. Instead of feeling like a failure and hating herself, she began to feel fully alive again. Her children responded generously by recognizing the shifts that she had made and acknowledging her as a vastly improved mother and a devoted grandmother.

If we keep this question in mind while planning our days, we will see that we actually have countless opportunities to add to our life force. Being around people and places we love and doing things that give us deep satisfaction, taking time to digest the events in our lives, being less busy, telling the truth, laughing a lot, eating right, exercising regularly, having long talks with those we love—these are among the best ways to nourish our vitality. Our life force thrives when we are completely engaged in the present moment.

We rob ourselves of energy when we dwell on the past. Mentally rehashing situations, events, and circumstances that we have no power to change diminishes our ability to be present here and now. Every time you think about what your parents failed to give you, the ways your ex-lover mistreated you, or how your best friend betrayed you, you zoom to the past, to the land of no return, and your vital energy drains away.

The Toltec tradition tells us that we surrender a portion of our life force when we dwell on any unhealed wounding event from our past. The unprocessed emotions surrounding these events burden us and weigh heavily on our hearts. They must be dealt with if we want access to all of our vitality. Ultimately, what we will find is that forgiveness is the key to reclaiming all the life force locked in past hurt.

• • •

Maggie and Sarah had already been best friends for five years when they landed jobs in the same advertising firm. Although they usually were assigned to different accounts, the two friends often helped each other by brainstorming ideas over lunch. Their enthusiasm and camaraderie had a big effect on all those around them, transforming the previously serious workplace into a place of energy and fun and vitality. But then the two friends had a falling-out that changed all of that.

One weekend Sarah and her husband invited Maggie over for a barbecue. Maggie said something to Sarah's husband that Sarah felt was a huge betrayal of their friendship and her confidence. Sarah asked Maggie to leave and didn't speak to her the rest of the weekend. The next Monday at work, the tension between the two was palpable. The resentment persisted as each woman dug in her heels and clung to her position.

The stone wall of silence remained in place for eighteen months. During that time the two had offices right next to each another but never spoke. When they attended meetings together they exchanged only cold glares. When one was acknowledged for her accomplishments, the other seethed with contempt. Sarah began to dread going to work each day. She felt unsafe expressing herself in Maggie's presence, and as a result her creativity and work performance diminished, along with her vitality.

Sarah was at her wit's end and considered looking for another job. She loved the company she worked for and remembered what going to work there used to feel like. When I encouraged her to look deeper, Sarah saw that the only thing standing in the way of her feeling that good again was the resentment she was holding toward Maggie. She realized that the grudge was costing her dearly. It was affecting her mood, her mental wellness, and even her performance at her job. When I asked Sarah this Right Question—"Is this resentment adding to your life force or is it robbing you of your energy?"—it became perfectly clear to her what she needed to do. Sarah made the courageous choice to let go of her grievance against Maggie.

The next day Sarah invited Maggie to lunch and told her that she was sorry for what had happened and asked for her forgiveness. They both cried and were able to express how hard it had been on each of them to carry this burden of resentment around—how difficult it had been to be so physically close to each other and yet so far from each other's hearts.

Not only did the two women have much more energy and excitement available to them, but the whole office celebrated the reconciliation of their differences. Everyone enjoyed the atmosphere of renewed trust, collaborative spirit, and freedom of expression that flowed in the office. Neither woman had realized how much their resentment had depleted the vitality of those around them.

It is a choice to give our precious energy away. It is a choice to hang on to our resentments or to forgive those who have disappointed us. Resentment robs us of our life force. It might be the biggest killer of the human spirit that exists today. We have the power to choose to give up the past, move on, and reclaim our energy now.

Asking this Right Question allows us to capture all the energy that's available to us in every moment. It challenges us to look at each of the choices we make every day to see whether they are feeding or depleting our internal flame. We can't make choices that weaken our flame and expect our fire to roar. Our life force is our connection to our passion and our vitality. When it burns brightly, we have the energy, the strength, and the confidence to meet our daily obligations and pursue our dreams. When our life force is strong we exude the brilliance and beauty of our true nature.

9

Will I Use This Situation as a Catalyst to Grow and Evolve or Will I Use It to Beat Myself Up?

Turning our dreams into realities means learning how to transmute the negative and turn it into the positive. This is a vitally important life skill that, when practiced, can transform pain into peace and turmoil into triumph. All of us have endured events and circumstances in our lives that have stopped us in our tracks and prevented us from moving forward. We've all experienced hardships, tragedies, and other setbacks that have made it difficult to see the beauty and rightness in all things. These events are inevitable. They are part of our human experience. While it's not possible for us to prevent unwanted life experiences from happening, it is possible to turn our emotional wounds into wisdom and

to use every event as a catalyst to bring us greater understanding.

As human beings we have the unique ability to
choose how we will interpret and digest each event that
takes place in our lives. We've all been blessed with the
very precious gift of free will. Free will provides us with
the power to choose how we will deal with our experiences. Free will enables us to use the events of our lives
to grow and evolve or to beat ourselves up.

This Right Question—"Will I use this situation as a
catalyst to grow and evolve or will I use it to beat myself
up?"—urges us to embrace the truth that life will inevitably bring us some difficult experiences. And they
aren't always our fault. When we come upon an incident
or event that brings with it pain, sadness, loss, or regret,
we don't want to hide or deny these feelings. We must
allow ourselves to feel our emotions, acknowledge our
hurt, and then make the decision to use this event to
make our lives better. We must examine the incident itself and see how we've interpreted it. Then we can
choose a new perspective.

Our perspectives shape our reality. A new, powerful
perspective can actually add value to our lives rather than
rob us of a future filled with love, dignity, and peace of

mind. This Right Question asks us to look at what happens to us from the perspective that every person and situation in our lives is behaving in exactly the way we need them to at every moment in time. A person cutting us off, delivering bad news, refusing to meet our needs; a child acting out to get our attention—if we ask ourselves, "What can I learn from this encounter? How can I use this to evolve and transform my life?" we will start to open up to new possibilities for our lives. The other option is to spend our time wondering, "What have I done to deserve this?" or "What am I doing wrong?" The first option will allow us to see viewpoints that we haven't been able to see before; the second will keep us trapped in the painful reality of being a victim. The latter reality gives us no choice other than to feel bad about who we are and then beat ourselves up. These are the two options that this Right Question offers us.

Everything in this life can be used to transform us, to bring us closer to our spiritual essence and our dreams. In other words, either we are using life in our favor or we are using it against ourselves. This is what is meant by the saying "Life is a teacher to the wise man and an enemy to the fool." By seeing life as a teacher, we transcend the pain and suffering we put on ourselves. And then we can spend our energy creating what we want rather than wasting it by rehashing the past.

This Right Question will immediately shift our perspective from one of self-doubt or recrimination to one of open-minded learning. It defuses the moment and moves our inquiries from proving how wrong the situation is to wondering how we can take a positive action and claim a positive result.

Our perspectives on situations color how we see others as well as ourselves. They act like a lens through which we view the world. If we commit to using every event, relationship, and experience as an opportunity to grow and learn, if we look for the ways in which each incident can support us in becoming the best human beings possible, we will most definitely see new possibilities in situations that might at first seem hopeless. Then we are able to extract vital wisdom from these events that will provide us with the fuel we need to overcome setbacks and move forward. When we are looking at life through this lens, we experience a whole new level of understanding. More important, when we ask this question, we move effortlessly toward the future we desire.

It's easy to get stuck in the drama of our present life circumstances and, instead of using an event as a catalyst to grow, to make whatever has happened to us mean something bad about ourselves and to use the situation as a way to beat ourselves up. Most of us don't need anyone to punish us, because we are constantly punishing ourselves. There are many, many ways to beat ourselves up and punish ourselves. We beat ourselves up by depriving ourselves of what we truly want or by acting out in ways that will ultimately hurt us—engaging in overwork or overeating. We beat ourselves up by indulging in behaviors that leave us feeling ashamed. We beat ourselves up every time we fail to acknowledge ourselves for the gains we have made. We beat ourselves up by rehashing an event over and over in our mind, analyzing why we didn't do it better and how we could have done it differently. We beat ourselves up by spending our precious energy trying to figure out how we could have avoided the situation altogether. It doesn't matter if it's a missed appointment or an unreturned phone call or the breakup of a relationship; we always have a choice to use each event to learn and grow or to use it against ourselves.

Lisa and Howard had been dating for nearly a year and had even begun to bring up the idea of moving in together. Lisa had fallen head over heels in love with Howard from the first moment she met him. He was charming, sexy, and very exciting to be around.

Howard had a way of keeping Lisa on her toes. She often wondered how he really felt about her. Throughout their relationship Lisa received many warning signs that perhaps Howard wasn't her man. He had a wandering eye and a fixation with gambling that made Lisa very uncomfortable. But Lisa stayed in the relationship, and together they went to couples counseling, hoping to work through their differences and sort out their priorities. The day finally came when Lisa heard from one of her girlfriends that Howard had been seeing another woman. Although she was devastated, Lisa ended the relationship immediately and never looked back.

In the weeks that followed, Lisa couldn't help thinking about all the warning signs she had ignored and the opportunities to date other men that she had missed while she was with Howard. She grieved the wasted year of her life, and all the time and energy she had spent investing in her future with Howard. Then one crisp winter morning as Lisa took her daily walk, she realized that she had a crucial choice to make in how she was relating to her situation. She could use her breakup with Howard to continue to beat herself up, or she could use it as a catalyst to grow and evolve and to move her closer to the relationship she desired.

Lisa took out her journal and feverishly began writing about all she had learned as a result of the year she had spent with Howard. Her list looked like this:

- I learned that I deserve to be with a man who is madly in love with me.

- I learned to trust my instincts and pay closer attention to the clues people give me about who they are.

- I learned that the most important thing I can do when I meet a man is to really look on the inside—to buy the book and not the cover.

- I learned not to compromise my values.

Because of her experience with Howard, Lisa was clearer than ever about what she wanted—and didn't want—in a man. This led Lisa to make a list of all the qualities she now knew were important to her in a man:

- Honesty

- Integrity

- Generosity

- Financial responsibility

- Kindness

Most of these qualities are things Lisa had never even thought to look for in a man. But thanks to her experience with Howard, Lisa now had greater clarity about what was truly important to her in the man she would choose as a life partner. By the time Lisa completed her lists, she had made a dramatic shift. She had made the choice to use her breakup with Howard to move her closer to the relationship she desired and to no longer use it to beat herself up. This shift left Lisa excited about her future and grateful for the role Howard had played in helping her clarify her desires.

When we are beating ourselves up, we have no access to the divine wisdom that can be extracted from sorrow and disappointment. The great Swiss psychologist Carl Jung said, "The gold is in the dark." It is our job to find the gold in every situation and use it to move us in the direction of our dreams. We are the designers. We are the ones who choose the lens through which we will view the world. When we're headed toward our goals and then "life happens," we must, in order to keep from getting detoured, ask this Right Question and make the powerful choice to use the event as an opportunity to grow. We must be brave enough to stand rooted in the wisdom that there are no accidents and that everything is exactly as it should be. It is precisely at the moments of greatest challenge that we need to look beyond what we can see and find a deeper meaning in them. When we find that deeper meaning, we will experience forgiveness and freedom from the events of our past. This alone will shift our perspective and give us access to a broader view of reality.

This Right Question is particularly useful when you are suffering. If you are suffering, you are certainly using something from your past or your present to beat yourself up. If you want to stop suffering, shift your perspective and ask yourself this important question: "How can I use what I am experiencing right now to grow and evolve?" This question offers you immediate relief and allows you to see your life as a work in progress. When you choose to see the events of your life as learning experiences, you automatically transform painful moments into enlightened ones. The great spiritual teacher Muktananda says,

"Use everything to your advantage." This is the hallmark of spiritual mastery. When we make the choice to use these moments to expand our understanding of ourselves and the world rather than to contract into self-pity or re-crimination, we make the jump from helplessness to power. Mastery is choosing to use the situations we find ourselves in rather than letting them use us.

All you need to do to radically change your life is to make the choice to see your triumphs and your tragedies as invitations to grow and evolve. Asking this Right Question propels you immediately into positive action, moving you toward greater understanding, clarity, and purpose.

10

Does This Choice Empower Me or Does It Disempower Me?

What does it mean to be empowered? To empower means to give or add power, to propel. When you're empowered you feel strong, alive, and clear, with a vibrant energy that runs through your body. When you make choices that empower you, you are thrust into the present moment. You experience a deep inner knowing that you are exactly where you need to be. When you feel empowered, you have access to higher levels of consciousness. Because you are choosing to move forward in a powerful way, your mind is quiet and void of its usual negative chatter. People who are empowered stand up for themselves and invite others to do the same. They are in a state of being where pure love—love of life, love of self, and love of others—abounds. They provide hope to those who shrink in the presence of everyday life. People who feel empowered are natural leaders who inspire those around them. This Right Question—"Does this choice empower me or does it disempower me?"—will give you the ability to access the state of empowerment any time you want it.

Sitting on my desk is a sign that reads, ARE YOU OVER YOUR SKIS? I keep it there as a reminder of what empowerment feels like. Being empowered means feeling the exhilaration of moving effortlessly down a mountain. It is a state of being in balance with the laws of nature, where you are giving all that you have—not holding on, not looking back, but staying keenly focused on where you want to go. For those of you who aren't skiers, one thing you quickly learn when you start skiing is that if your weight is not over your skies you will be thrown off balance. New skiers typically try to lean back—into the hill—thinking that this is where they will find safety. But if you try to go down the mountain leaning into the hill you are actually much more likely to take a spill and land on your rear.

To stay on your feet and have a smooth ride you must go against your natural instincts to hold on. In the forward position you will actually find solid ground—a safe, fluid movement that will allow you to flow down the hill with great ease and joy. This is exactly what empowerment feels like. When you are moving full speed in the direction of your desires, taking action, letting go, and being in perfect alignment with the universe, you are empowering yourself and your life.

Asking this Right Question will quickly move you out of the past and into the present moment, because you can actually *feel* the experience of empowerment inside your body. You know that your choices empower you when they leave you feeling strong and secure inside. You know you have made a disempowering choice when you feel insecure, inadequate, and resigned.

For several years now, through my coaching institute, I have been training people on how to facilitate my work and become Integrative Coaches. One of my coaches-in-training, Suzanna, is a stunning woman in her late forties. She emanates warmth, love, and compassion. When Suzanna first began her training, I expected her to create a thriving full-time coaching practice in no time at all.

But after six months of struggling to get her coaching practice off the ground, it became obvious that something was keeping Suzanna from achieving this goal. Although she is a remarkable woman and a brilliant coach, she frequently shortchanges herself by showing up late for calls or looking harried and distracted during meetings. I finally sat down with Suzanna in order to look at where in her life she was making choices that were leaving her disempowered rather than empowered.

As we began to talk, the first thing that came to Suzanna's mind was the fact that she was holding down three part-time jobs while also trying to build her coaching practice. Although the income helped her to make ends meet while her husband was working to develop a new business, Suzanna said that at the end of her long days she was left feeling tired and resentful.

I asked Suzanna if the choices she was making with regard to her career were empowering her. "Clearly," she said, "they are not." In fact, they were robbing her of peace of mind and making her less effective in every area of her life, including her coaching practice. Each day she grew more and more resigned to living a life that was less than what she truly desired. Her choices were even having a negative impact on her relationship with her husband, John, whom she adored.

I then asked her, "Of the three jobs you are working right now, which one really empowers you?" For
Suzanna, this was an easy question to answer. Suzanna's
first love was coaching. She said that she would like
nothing better than to focus all of her time, talents, and
efforts on developing a thriving coaching practice. I
asked Suzanna to make a list of all the disempowering
choices she had been making that were leading her further away from her goal. Her list looked like this:

- Instead of devoting my energies to developing my
  coaching career, I am working three jobs and as a
  result I feel scattered and exhausted.

- I haven't been taking care of myself, so people
  don't find what I have to offer appealing.

- I overcommit and then use lack of time as an
  excuse for why I don't promote and grow my
  coaching practice.

I then asked Suzanna to make a list of what she would
need to do in order to be available for a full-time coaching practice. Her second list looked like this:

- I would need to let go of the other jobs I am holding down to supplement my income.

- I would need to devote an hour each day to taking care of myself.

- I would need to spend one hour each day talking to people and promoting my Integrative Coaching practice.

Since Suzanna was committed to having a life that inspired and empowered her, she made the courageous choice to take these actions. Before she picked up the phone to call her employers, Suzanna read the sign I had her post above her computer, which read, WILL THIS ACTION EMPOWER ME OR DISEMPOWER ME? Suzanna knew what the answer was. She made the empowering choices and immediately quit two of her three part-time jobs. In addition, she adopted a regular practice of self-care that included daily exercise and quiet time.

Over the next few days after taking these empowering actions, Suzanna received several phone calls—totally out of the blue—from people with whom she had once spoken about Integrative Coaching. It seemed miraculous to Suzanna that when she made the choice to empower herself, everything she wanted effortlessly showed up. Taking on these new clients would almost completely compensate for the income she had just given up. Within the first month she gained four additional clients and was well on her way to reaching her goal.

Suzanna could have chosen to play it safe and continue giving up her dream for a false sense of security, but if she had, she would not be living the life she is today. When we are empowered we boldly move forward. And when we're disempowered we hold back, trying to cling to whatever we believe will keep us safe. When we are feeling disempowered we look to others to give us our sense of self-worth. Just close your eyes after you have made a choice to disempower yourself and you will be able to hear your negative internal chatter carrying you to a state of resignation. Our internal dialogue is infused with the past—with all our failures, fears, mistakes, and re-grets. Disempowerment leaves us feeling weak and unsure. Disempowering choices, repeated often enough, lead to hopelessness. Our hopelessness then leads to resignation, which leads to mistrust. And if we can't trust ourselves to make choices that are in our highest and best interest, whom can we trust?

• • •

Bette is twenty-three years old and fresh out of college. She was looking forward to finding a steady job and creating a lifestyle that would honor and nurture her. One night while Bette was out with some friends she met a young man named Nick. Nick came on strong and told her all the things women love to hear—that she was smart, beautiful, and fun. What Nick didn't know was that Bette had made a decision earlier that month not to date anybody until she found the right job. Her past had shown her that relationships took up a lot of her time, and she had decided she couldn't afford to divert her energy if she was serious about her job search. Yet the day after they met, when Nick called her and invited her to meet him for lunch, Bette said yes. Instead of saying no and keeping to her commitment of spending the day working on her résumé, Bette made a choice that would ultimately disempower her and take her off track.

For the next month Bette grew more deeply involved with Nick, and two or three times a week she would make the choice to set aside her career goals in order to have a rendezvous with him. Each time Bette did something other than what she had promised herself, she unknowingly disempowered herself. Four months later, Bette's relationship with Nick had ended and she was still jobless. But now, instead of being jobless and enthusiastic about her life, Bette was unemployed and feeling powerless and resigned. How easy it is to disempower ourselves! Seemingly innocent choices made in the heat of the moment can rob us of hope for the future and diminish our dreams. Every time we tell ourselves one thing and do another, we disempower ourselves.

You can use this Right Question at any time, in any circumstance, to determine whether your thoughts are leaving you in a state of empowerment or disempowerment. Our thoughts are the designers of our destinies. One of the most important shifts we can each make is to examine the quality of our thoughts and use this question to raise the level of our thinking. Researchers tell us that we think approximately sixty thousand thoughts per day, and I would venture to say that most of these thoughts are negative. This negative internal chatter might sound like "I look so tired today" or "I look horrible in these pants." It might show up when you hang up the phone from a business call and think to yourself, "I should have said this" or "I shouldn't have been such a pushover." When you catch yourself listening to any such chatter, you can stop, take a moment, and ask yourself, "Does listening to this internal dialogue right now empower me or disempower me?" If you see that you are disempowered by the chatter in your mind, *stop listening!*

You are either empowering or disempowering yourself in your daily behaviors. Before you start to eat something, you can ask yourself, "Will eating this food empower me or disempower me?" Before you go to buy something you can ask, "Will this purchase empower me or disempower me?" Of course, you need to make sure you have your goals and dreams firmly in your awareness as you do this. Buying a new outfit may seem like an empowering choice in the moment, but if your goal is to save money you would need to ask yourself, "Given my commitment to save money, would buying this outfit empower me?" Or if your goal is to have a more loving, supportive relationship with your spouse and he or she has asked you to curb your spending habits, you would want to ask yourself, "Given my commitment to having a better relationship with my spouse, would buying this outfit empower me or disempower me?" You can ask yourself this question if you are thinking about not telling a friend what you're upset about or missing your son's school picnic. If you find yourself tempted to run just one more errand on your way home, knowing that doing so will make you late for dinner, you can ask, "Is this an empowering choice?"

This question challenges you once again to make your actions conscious. Before making any choice, ask yourself this Right Question and look deeply within for the answer. You will often find that just by checking in with yourself and asking, "Does this choice leave me feeling weak or strong?" you will be able to see whether the action you are about to take will empower you or disempower you. At every moment we are making choices that empower us or we are making choices that do just the opposite. Empowerment is free; it costs nothing. It's a choice that only you can make.

11

Is This an Act of Self-Love or Is It an Act of Self-Sabotage?

The question "Is this an act of self-love or is it an act of self-sabotage?" is one you must consistently ask yourself if you are committed to having all that you want and all that you deserve. When you love yourself you feel worthy and deserving of claiming the gifts of this world. Self-love gives you peace of mind and balance. Self-love gives you self-respect and the ability to respect others. It gives you the confidence to stand up and ask for what you want. Self-love is the main ingredient in a successful, fulfilled life.

I believe that loving who we are is one of the most difficult yet vitally important tasks that each of us is given in this lifetime. Loving ourselves means loving *all* of who we are—the brilliant and beautiful, the flawed and foolish, the selfless and self-absorbed, the courageous and fearful. It means loving, honoring, and accepting the totality of our humanity. It means cherishing ourselves and appreciating our individuality and our uniqueness. When we choose self-love, we claim our greatness. When we love ourselves, we accept ourselves as a brilliant piece of architecture that is whole unto itself rather than a project under construction that constantly needs to be fixed, changed, and rebuilt.

Loving ourselves means loving what we believe, loving where we came from, loving our quirks and our handicaps. Each of us comes into this world with particular sets of strengths and weaknesses, and since these aspects of ourselves are more than likely not going to go away, our job is to embrace them all by finding compassion and understanding for the imperfections in our human selves.

Self-love makes us acutely aware of our own needs and supports us in doing whatever it takes to meet these needs on a regular basis. When we love ourselves fully and freely, something magical happens. We teach others, without using words, how to love themselves. We become models of self-love—for our children, our family members, our friends, and our communities. We teach them not only that self-love is a good choice to make but that it is really the only choice. When we give ourselves the gift of self-love, all those around us are touched in our presence and feel deeper levels of love for themselves. Most important, when we love ourselves, we freely allow ourselves to experience the joys and gifts of this world.

What does it mean to choose self-love? It means making choices that you feel good about on a day-to-day basis and being able to look yourself in the eye and know that you did what was best for yourself. It means being proud of your choices and your actions. Loving yourself means making choices that allow you to care for the important person that you are.

Each of us is given only one temple to be responsible for, and we are living in it. If I leave my temple so that I can take care of yours, and mine burns down, I didn't do my job in this world. But if I take care of my own temple, I will have the resources to support you with yours. So it is essential to think of yourself—your body, your mind, and your spirit—as your very sacred temple, to honor and care for. Then you will understand that even the tiniest unconscious act becomes one of self-sabotage that will add to your self-loathing instead of your self-esteem.

When I first began using this question with clients, I started by asking them to consider whether their choices were acts of self-love or self-hatred. I quickly discovered that most people have an understandable aversion to the concept of self-hatred. Even though my clients could see that their choices were not acts of self-love, the idea that they were doing something that showed that they actually hated themselves was too difficult for them to digest. I admit, the term *self-hatred* is quite strong, but from my perspective every act of self-sabotage is an act of self-hatred. If you love yourself, you will make choices that are in your highest and best interest. You will take the time to think deeply about what makes you feel good about yourself. Since this book is based on the concept that the truth will set you free, I feel compelled to support you in seeing, as an act of self-love, how cruel it is to make choices that do not support you in creating the life you want.

As we all know, when you love someone or something, you look out for their best interests. You spend time caring for them out of your genuine desire that they feel good. If you are committed to your children's education, you don't go out and find a bad school to send them to. If you want them to be healthy and strong, you don't feed them foods packed with sugar, fat, and cholesterol. You take time and care in making choices on their behalf. You bring your awareness to your choices. That is what this Right Question asks you to do for yourself. It asks you to stop and take the time to become aware of what you are consciously and unconsciously committed to, and then make sure the decisions that you make, your choices, are really choices that will lead you to your desired destination.

When we engage in self-sabotaging behaviors, we are choosing from our lowest selves rather than our highest. We allow unhealthy underlying commitments to direct us away from our desired destinations. Consequently, we go through our days in a state of distress and unease. When we are self-sabotaging, when we deny ourselves our own love, we are scared to death of what other people think of us. We become masters of disguise, always trying to conceal the things we hate about ourselves. We give off the message to those around us that not only don't we matter, but they don't matter, either. When we are self-sabotaging, we deny ourselves the right to have what we want and we unconsciously give other people the false perception that it's okay to deprive themselves of their dreams, too.

Remember, each choice we make moves us either toward our goals or away from them. We can rest assured that if we are not moving in the direction of what we say we want, we are sabotaging ourselves somewhere. Often it is difficult for us to see or admit to self-sabotaging behaviors because they are painful to look at, and it's even more painful to take responsibility for them. We come up with elaborate ways to avoid confronting our self-destruction. We blame our parents, our spouses, our circumstances, our governments, or the universe for not supplying us with all the goodies we deserve. We don't stop to examine the choices and behaviors we make that have contributed to our situation and have led us astray.

James is a great example of how we lead ourselves astray. James came to me hoping to create a more intimate relationship with his wife, Sallie. He longed to feel the love and connection that they had experienced at the beginning of their seven-year marriage. I asked James to see if he could identify choices he had made in his marriage that had interfered with his desire for intimacy with Sallie. James took this task to heart, but in spite of his eagerness, after weeks of looking he couldn't put his finger on any such choices.

Then one evening while waiting for Sallie to finish up with a business meeting, James decided to go to a nearby restaurant and eat an early dinner. He found a table at an outdoor cafe and did what he automatically did every time he was in a public place: he began looking at all the women who passed by. James loved watching women. He enjoyed admiring all their different shapes and sizes, and he especially liked fantasizing about how it might feel to be with one of them. But then, in a moment of truth, James realized that what he usually considered to be a harmless pastime was actually an act of self-sabotage. Watching and fantasizing about other women was one way to keep himself distracted and distant from his wife.

Choosing to watch other women actually robbed him of feeling excited about Sallie. James realized that this choice was not only disrespectful to her but clearly taking him in the opposite direction from where he wanted to go. James described his choice as an act of self-sabotage because it clearly depleted his vital energy and led him further away from his goal of being closer to Sallie.

Looking at other women kept James involved in fantasy rather than in the reality of his life with Sallie.

By asking himself this question and being courageous enough to hear the answer, James was encouraged to keep searching for the subtle ways in which he sabotaged himself and his marriage. His list looked like this:

- I blatantly admire other women, even in my wife's presence.

- I make Sallie wrong for not being like the women I have just fantasized about.

- I look to friends and co-workers for deep personal connections rather than seeking them with my wife.

- I withhold intimacy from Sallie and allow little resentments to build between us.

After making this list, James began to see that he could choose to stop these behaviors and use the energy that he had used watching women to come up with creative ways to be more intimate with his wife. Realizing that the choices he had made in the past had sabotaged the level of intimacy in his marriage, James made a list of new choices he could make, acts of self-love that would enrich him and his marriage. His second list looked like this:

- I could write down all the things I love, appreciate, and admire about Sallie.

- I could find exciting ways to be intimate with Sallie.

- I could spend ten minutes a day remembering times when I felt deeply connected to and intimate with Sallie.

- I could write cards to Sallie expressing my desire to have with her the most passionately intimate relationship I could imagine.

James could see that taking any of these actions would be an act of self-love, because each of them would allow him to feel better about his behavior toward Sallie. Deep inside, he knew he was committed to distancing himself from Sallie because of his fears of intimacy and thus engaged in behaviors that made him feel ashamed of himself. When he felt that shame, he didn't want to let Sallie—or anyone else, for that matter—close to him because he felt so bad about his own actions. What's important to know is that every time we act in a way that is against our stated desires, we break out in guilt, shame, or disappointment in ourselves. And naturally we keep people at a distance so they won't see what we so painfully feel. Until James made the choice to stop the behaviors that made him feel so bad about himself, he was never going to be able to have the relationship he said he wanted with Sallie.

Self-sabotage comes in many forms. Every time we allow a momentary distraction to pull us away from our dreams, every time we compare ourselves with another and come up short, and every time we look at our lives and think, "This isn't it," we have committed an act of self-sabotage. Every time we go unconscious and listen to our negative inner dialogue sing its same old song for the thousandth time, and every time we beat ourselves up for not being perfect, we are choosing self-sabotage over self-love.

We self-sabotage by paying reverence to our "should"s instead of honoring the wishes of our hearts. We all have so many "should"s that stand in the way of loving ourselves completely: I *should* think of others first; I *should* be more flexible; I *should* be happy eating carrots when what I really want is a piece of pie. It's so easy to not like ourselves because of these "should"s, but it is our job—the sacred task to which we've been assigned—to learn to love the person that we are, as we are, in the moment. Self-love does not come from writing a book, or from making a million dollars, or from buying a new house. Self-esteem comes from the little loving choices we make every day—the choices we make that tell us, "You are important. You are a good person. You deserve to take care of yourself. You matter."

I believe with all my heart that this is the most difficult task most of us have before us. When we truly are in the divine presence of our own humanity, we naturally make choices that reflect love of our deepest selves and give ourselves the gifts we so fully deserve. How we feel about ourselves now is a result of all the choices we have made in the past. So if you don't like the way you feel about yourself, you have the power to change it.

What if attaining happiness and fulfillment was as simple as going to bed at night after making a list of all the things you did that day that fed your self-esteem and waking up the next morning asking yourself, "How am I going to love and honor myself today?" What if the message of all the ancient gurus, the spiritual teachings, the self-help books, and all the transformational techniques we've created came down to teaching us how to give ourselves the love we try to get from others? What if all there is to do is to love ourselves completely and make new choices today, choices that are an expression of self-love? Before making a choice, ask yourself, "Would someone who loves themselves make this choice? Is this action an expression of someone who honors and cherishes themselves?" Both of these questions will bring you back to the simple question "Is this an act of self-love or is it an act of self-sabotage?"

12

Is This an Act of Faith or Is It an Act of Fear?

Every important choice we make is being guided by one of two places: either it is an act of faith or it is an act of fear. Faith opens the door to a new future. It allows us to take new routes and explore different avenues. When we are grounded in faith, we have the courage to travel to destinations we've never visited. This extremely potent question—"Is this an act of faith or is it an act of fear?"—supports us in making choices from our highest selves, from the part of us that is deeply connected to all that is and all that will be. When we are making choices that are sourced by our spiritual essence and are grounded in faith, we experience unbounded freedom.

Faith is a friend by our side. When we allow it in, faith

acts as the floor beneath our feet. When we make choices rooted in faith, we trust that there is a power, an unseen force, guiding us. When we have faith, we know that we are being taken care of. Faith gives us the ability to look beyond our immediate circumstances and imagine brave new choices for the future. Faith means trusting in something beyond what we know. Having faith that we are part of a bigger whole allows us to melt away our separateness. Faith gives us strength and reassurance and leaves us bathed in the wisdom that we are never alone.

Faith is the foundation for a spiritual life. When we make the choice to act from faith rather than fear, we are able to view the world from a higher perspective. Faith invites us to believe in something we cannot see, feel, or know. When our actions are based on faith, we are choosing to put our trust in something besides our fears.

Fear, on the other hand, keeps us rooted in the past. Fear of the unknown, fear of abandonment, fear of rejection, fear of not having enough, fear of not being enough, fear of the future—all these fears and more keep us trapped, repeating the same old patterns and making the same choices over and over again. Fear prevents us from moving outside the comfort—or even the familiar discomfort—of what we know. It's nearly impossible to achieve our highest vision for our lives as long as we are being guided by our fears.

Our fears tell us what we can and cannot do. They tell us to play small and be safe. Our fears cause us to try desperately to hold on to habits and behaviors even when they no longer serve us. The root of all our repetitive negative patterns is fear. Fear keeps us going around and around in circles, never allowing us to envision an exit from lives that bind and defeat us.

What are we afraid of? We are afraid that life won't bring us what we want or think we need. We fear that if we try and fail, it will hurt too much. Or maybe we're afraid that if we do succeed we'll feel guilty and won't be able to handle it. We fear that if we stand up and claim our piece of the world, we will be rejected or abandoned by our friends and families. We fear that our lives will become unmanageable and we will lose control. Any time we do something that is inconsistent with our past—that is different from who we've been or who we think ourselves to be—we are confronted with our fears.

Yet if we continue to make choices from a place of fear, we will miss vital opportunities and guarantee ourselves a future that is no more than a continuation of our past. If we are really honest with ourselves, we will see that many of our actions and choices arise out of the fear that losing what we already have—even if we don't like it—will be worse than not getting what we want. Our fear drives us to take a job we don't want because we're afraid we won't have enough money. Our fear may keep us in a dead-end relationship because we're scared we won't find anyone else, or it may lead us to make choices that dishonor ourselves because we're afraid another opportunity won't come our way. When fear is in control of our choices, we are left with few options. Fear fuels self-doubt and internal criticism. Fear destroys dreams and exterminates possibilities.

Fear shuts us down, while faith opens us up. Our fears are made up of our anger, pain, worries, resentments, and insecurities; faith is made up of hope, possibility, trust, and an inner belief in the benevolence of the universe. Recently I worked with a wonderful woman who had a long history of suffering in her intimate relationships. What Leslie wanted more than anything else was to have a loving, nurturing relationship, and recently she had met someone who appeared to be the perfect man. Even though Jacob wasn't really her type, he was emotionally available, loving, honest, and committed. For months Leslie tried to be open to having the relationship work out. She had spent years in and out of different relationships and felt that she had finally come to a place where she could settle down. But after eight months with Jacob, Leslie was discontent and torn inside because she so desperately wanted it to work out. The question she kept asking herself was, "Is there something wrong with me, or is he just not the one?" Leslie was confused and didn't know whether she should further commit to this man or break up with him altogether.

I had Leslie close her eyes, and I asked her, "If you had complete faith in the universe and in your future, what would you do?" In an instant Leslie knew that she would tell Jacob that even though she loved him very much, she wasn't able to choose to pursue a relationship with him at this time. I then asked Leslie to write down all the other things faith would say. Her list looked like this:

- Faith would say, "Jacob has brilliantly prepared me for my soul mate to come into my life."

- Faith would say, "I don't have to live in lack anymore."

- Faith would say, "I can trust that there is a bigger plan for me even though I can't see it."

- Faith would say, "Let go."

- Faith would say, "There is someone who will love and care for me more deeply than Jacob."

Then I asked her to write down what fear would say. Her second list looked like this:

- Fear would say, "I won't ever find anyone better."

- Fear would say, "I'll wind up all alone if I don't stay with Jacob."

- Fear would say, "There must be something wrong with me and that's why I'm not content with Jacob."

- Fear would say, "There is something wrong with me that prevents me from making long-term relationships work."

- Fear would say, "Hold on to Jacob, because having someone is better than having no one."

When Leslie was done writing her lists, she could see that the only fair and right choice to make was to end her relationship with Jacob. She clearly saw that she had stayed in it more out of fear that there was no one else and less out of faith that Jacob was the partner she was meant to find. Leslie recognized that one of the reasons all her relationships ended so badly was that fear kept her in them longer than was good for her and she always wound up doing something drastic, leaving both herself and her partner wounded.

We have to ask ourselves, "Where is my faith right now? Is my faith in my fears? Am I placing my faith in the idea that I'm not going to get what I want? Or am I placing my faith in the perfection of the universe? Do I have faith that I will be guided to the circumstances that will give me exactly what I need?"

Most of us misplace our faith. We have more faith in our pain, our past, and our negative beliefs than we do in our innate right to be happy. We have faith in being a victim; we have faith that we are going to come

up short or get cheated or that life won't work out for us. We don't trust that our needs will be met. We don't trust that we'll have everything we want. When we place our faith in our fears, we remain closed and shut off from the very things we desire the most. When we have faith in our negative beliefs, in our flaws, and in our insecurities, we rob ourselves of the opportunity to grow and change and blossom into the divine beings that we were meant to be. Asking ourselves this question will immediately expose how much or how little we trust the world.

When we choose to live a faith-based life, our first task is to resign as general manager of the universe. Faith asks us to surrender control of our lives. Surrender is an act of courage. It is a divine path that gives us access to realities beyond what we know. To surrender and live a faith-based life is to acknowledge the divine nature of the universe. To surrender affirms that we trust in a higher power to tend to our needs and guide us in the direction of our heart's desires. Surrender is an act of faith; it's a gift that you give yourself. It's saying, "Even though I feel scared or I'm not sure where I am going, I trust that all will turn out in my highest and best interest." Faith equals trust. Faith offers us hope and opportunity and promise. If we choose to live in faith, we will be blessed with the support and the partnership of the universe.

13

Am I Choosing from My Divinity or Am I Choosing from My Humanity?

This Right Question carries with it the power to shift your entire life. Asking "Am I choosing from my divinity or am I choosing from my humanity?" can lift you out of the smallness of your individual reality and deliver you to a place where you have the power and the wisdom to transcend any circumstance or human struggle. When you ask yourself this question, you immediately get to shift from a conditional life based on reacting to the world around you to the eternal, secure foundation of a life grounded in divine truth.

Divine consciousness and human consciousness coexist within each of us. Most of us are unaware that although we are human, we have access to higher levels of consciousness at every moment of our lives. When we access these higher levels of consciousness, we open up to a divine experience that alters the way we see our lives and the trials and tribulations of our everyday human existence. Asking this Right Question opens the door for us to experience realms of reality that we may never have visited before.

When we look at our lives and our experiences through the divine perspective, we can suddenly see other views not available to us when we are looking only through the lens of our own humanness. When we make the conscious choice to rise above our egos, our fears, and the limitations of our own individual realities, we become privy to information and ideas that aren't available to us when we are looking through the narrow limits of our human eyes.

When we are looking from a divine perspective, we intuitively know the actions to take that will benefit others as well as ourselves. This means we have to consider more than just our own reality and be open to other people's perspectives as well. We've all heard the expression that there are three sides to every story— yours, theirs, and mine. When we allow ourselves to view all of these realities at once, we transcend the limitations of our humanity and awaken to the divine perspective. What we can accomplish through our human efforts pales in comparison to what we can accomplish when we allow in the divine.

Many of us don't even realize that we have a choice about which aspect of ourselves we will use as the foundation upon which we build our lives. So it's no wonder that the majority of us allow our lower selves—our fears, our egos, our cravings, and our humanity—to influence our choices, guide our actions, and run the show. Our humanity is the part of us that is driven by survival and fear. It's the part that struggles and toils, manipulates and controls in order to get what we think will bring us happiness. Our human selves crave acknowledgment and want to take credit for what we create in our lives. Our humanity clings to strategies and agendas because it doesn't feel safe enough to place its trust in the divine order of life. When we make choices from the perspective of our humanity, we eventually wind up feeling powerless, depressed, and exhausted.

It's important to know that our humanity is not "wrong." In fact, it is beautiful. In order to live our greatest lives we must make peace with our human selves, for only then are we able to surrender our lives to the divine. Our human self is the keeper of many of our gifts, but it is also filled with limitations, excuses, and self-serving agendas.

This Right Question gives us a choice about which aspect of ourselves we will allow to direct the course of our lives, our daily choices, and our moment-to-moment awareness. It gives us the power to choose: "Shall my divinity or my humanity run the show today?"

When I first brought this question to her attention, Shelley was at her wit's end. A divorced mother, she was trying to manage a career as a high school teacher, another career as the mother of two teenage boys, and a relationship with a man she loved. Always in a state of being overwhelmed, Shelley often felt annoyed, frustrated, and discontent. The phony smile on her face left those around her feeling deceived and confused, because while she smiled at them nonstop, she was communicating in an overly harsh tone all the things that she thought needed to be done differently. She ordered people around from the moment she woke up until she laid her head down at night. Her days were spent trying to figure out how she could get more money from her ex-husband, how she could keep her boyfriend interested in her, and how she could get her two sons to do everything on their activity lists—including homework—on time and without complaining. Even Shelley recognized that she was turning into a control freak, and because of this she was beginning to hate herself and her life.

One day after a blowout with another teacher at work, Shelley ran into the teachers' lounge and burst into tears. The dam broke, and she could no longer hold it all together. Suddenly in the presence of all her pain, discontent, and frustration, Shelley saw for the first time that she really needed help. When she showed up at one of my seminars, I asked Shelley to make a wish list of all the things she wanted in her life. Her list looked like this:

- I want peace of mind.

- I want to trust that those around me will take care of themselves.

- I want to have some time every day to do something for me.

- I want to know that I have help and support.

- I want to feel that I am connected to the rest of the world.

- I want to make a difference in the world.

As we read over her list, it was easy to see that Shelley was dealing with one of the most common human struggles. Shelley was feeling isolated, alone, scared, and completely disconnected from the rest of the world. Her life had turned into the exact thing she had wanted to avoid. She had become just another individual trying to survive life rather than the great woman she aspired to be who made a difference in the world and was a highly respected, contributing member of society.

I asked Shelley to consider the choices she had made over the past few years and to ask herself whether they were made from the place of her humanity or from her higher self—her divinity. At first she looked at me like I was nuts. The concept of divinity was simply not on her radar. But I pointed out to her that every choice we make has its source either in our lower selves, our humanity, or in our higher selves, our divinity. When I explained it in that way, it took less than a minute for Shelley to realize that the vast majority of her choices were made from fear, out of a reaction from her past, and were made with only her individual concerns in mind, without consideration for the greater contribution she held for the world. I explained to her that such a response isn't "bad" and that in fact most of us automatically choose from our own individual interests; that's only human. I assured Shelley that it is our natural instinct to survive, and that if we are not reminded and vigilant we all fall naturally back into the automatic programming of me, mine, myself, and I—the first language of our humanity.

After Shelley had taken some time to consider our conversation, I asked her if she would be willing to look at her life from a higher perspective. Shelley was more than willing to do so. I asked her to close her eyes and get in touch with the highest vision she holds for herself. As the tears rolled down her cheeks, Shelley remembered herself as a young woman who had set out to change the world. She reconnected with her deep desire to become an inspiring teacher and write books to support other teachers in becoming more effective and making more of an impact on today's youth. Long hidden were her dreams of having a warm and wonderful family life filled with love, sharing, and laughter.

After many minutes Shelley stood in the presence of the future that had governed so many of her choices as a

young adult and saw how after a few disappointments—
the breakup of her marriage and other life events—
those dreams had become only a dim memory.

I then suggested that Shelley take a silent lunch break
and give herself permission to imagine that she was again
a young woman standing at the doorway to her most
magnificent life. I asked her to come back with a list of all
the choices she would make if she knew that she was a divine being who had the power to create magic in her life
and the lives of others. I asked her to dream big and imagine that anything was possible. The question at hand was
which actions she would take if her divinity was guiding
her rather than her humanity. Her list looked like this:

- I would wake up in the morning and take ten
  minutes of silence and prayer to connect with my
  higher self.

- I would create a mission statement for myself to
  remind me of my dream to impact the teachers of
  the world.

- I would join an organization of teachers and go to
  at least two conferences a year, even if I had to
  pay for them myself.

- I would enroll my boys in my vision to impact the quality of education and ask them to be my partners.

- I would ask my boyfriend to spend an hour a week with me supporting me in finding opportunities that are in alignment with my vision.

- I would let the principal and all the other teachers at my school know what I am really committed to.

- I would share my vision with my students.

- I would rally a team of teachers who have the same or similar goals and form a support group so that we could all fulfill our missions.

- I would find an outstanding summer job to supplement my income.

In less than an hour Shelley was shining bright—inspired, energized, and deeply rooted in her heart. Her hostility had disappeared, and in its place were feelings of love and appreciation.

Weeks later Shelley let me know that her understanding of the distinction between human choices and divine choices had totally transformed her reality, as well as the realities of those around her. Her children felt in-spired and more loved and accepted; her boyfriend was enthused that Shelley had found her way back home to her highest vision. Shelley said she felt as though she were being guided by something much bigger than her-self. "The greatest gift I have received from this ques-tion," she proclaimed, "is that I now feel connected to the greater whole."

I'm going to assert that 90 percent of us let our human selves direct the course of our lives, simply because we have forgotten that we have the power to choose a higher path. Even those of us who have done a lot of inner work or have a daily spiritual practice can't take for granted that our actions will automatically be guided by our divinity, because our human tendencies run so deep. As we use this question it is important to under-stand that making choices from our divinity is a practice that must be deliberately cultivated each day and in every moment. For most of us, our default way of being in the world is to operate from our humanity.

We can all experience success when we make choices from our humanity. It is certainly possible to produce results and find fulfillment while making choices from our human selves. I have proved this many times my-self. But I also know from personal experience that when we allow ourselves to tap into the divine, when we make the choice to reach for guidance and power that is beyond our own individual selves, what comes of it is greater than anything we, with our human lim-itations, could possibly have created. Whether it's a business, a relationship, or a matter of parenting, when we allow ourselves to step out of our smaller selves, greater things result. When we are attached to solving a problem through our humanity, our choices are very limited. But when we surrender the situation to the di-vine, the answer can come to us in many ways. We can suddenly see an answer that was there all along. We have all had the serendipitous experience of someone sending us an article that provides just the answer we were looking for. Or we run into someone we haven't seen in a while and discover that they have the exact skill or connection we need to move our business for-ward. The divine is unlimited—it operates beyond human limits—and when we choose to look at our lives through divine eyes, we see there are many options available to us.

• • •

This was certainly true for Mark, a man in his late fifties who is now retired. In his youth Mark was a hotshot Miami attorney—a force to be reckoned with. He was known for his genius and his ruthlessness. He was thought of as strong willed, bright, and in charge. He used his force and his wisdom to bully people. His knowledge of the law propelled him to the top of his field. When he wasn't tending to his clients' business, he was taking care of his own vendettas. His driving commitment was to get even with the people he felt had wronged him. Mark spent twenty-five years of his life making choices from his humanity, not knowing that these choices would ultimately rob him of his life force, disempower him, and take away his right to live a happy life. In fact, his attachment to his personal battles cost him his passion and fulfillment.

Then one day, at the conclusion of yet another battle, Mark broke down. He realized that it no longer mattered if he won or lost. At the end of any of his lawsuits he was left feeling drained, tired, and unfulfilled. There was no glory, no real resolution, and no contentment to be found in these shallow pursuits. In a moment of grace Mark woke up and realized that his victories were hollow and his losses devastating. He could no longer continue making choices from that place inside him that was interested only in getting even.

In a grand gesture, Mark closed his law practice and put away his law degree. Shamed by his obsessive behavior, Mark turned to a higher source for guidance. To his great surprise, the answers he sought came easily. He saw that there was a greater source of justice in the world than himself and that the divine path was the road to glory and the human path was the road to grief. He realized that when he stepped back from his grievances and took the high road, he served not only himself but his entire family and his community at large.

I asked Mark to make a list of what living from his humanity had brought him. His list looked like this:

- Financial security

- A great reputation

- Success

- Stress

- Aggravation

- Emotional turmoil

- Inner conflict

- Anger

- Grief

- Disappointment

- Resignation

- Emptiness

As he made the list, Mark could see that even though he was an outward success, he was an inner mess. He learned that if he accepted that there was a power greater, wiser, and more just than his own—and if he made his choices based in that power—he got rewards he had never even imagined. I then asked Mark to list what he would have in his life if he chose from his divinity. His list looked like this:

- Peace of mind

- Self-esteem

- More time to spend on community projects

- More time with my family

- Time and energy to be creative and productive

- A more loving heart

- A greater appreciation for my time and energy

Mark began to take a wider view of his life and his options. He now lives each day with the understanding that as humans we have so much potential to grow, expand, and contribute to the lives of those we come in contact with, and we have only a limited amount of time in which to do it. He learned the hard way that when we spend our time criticizing, blaming, judging, and making the world around us wrong, we are in fact choosing to live at a level of consciousness where grief resides and discontent breeds. He shared with me the wisdom that his experience gave him: when we are spending time on the little picture, we have no time left to devote to the big picture. The big picture includes not only ourselves but also the world around us. Mark understood that choosing to act from his divinity might mean that sometimes he has to turn the other cheek or give up his position. The big picture calls on us to understand that there are a lot of unconscious people in the world acting in ways that violate others' well-being.

• • •

Once you decide to use this Right Question, the first step is to make a commitment to taking the high road and allow yourself to be guided by whatever power you believe exists. It can be God, Spirit, the universe, love, nature, or the highest aspect of yourself. Then make a list of what would be available to you if you allowed your life to be directed by this source, if you allowed this source to do things for you that you alone could not do. I did this years ago, when I first made the commitment to allow my actions to be guided by my highest self. It was important for me to write down all the benefits I would receive if I made the choice to step out of my humanness. I keep this list close to me so that whenever I am pulled to make a choice that will ultimately not serve the greater whole, I can read it and return to that divine place within myself. Here's my list of what I receive when I allow my divinity to guide me:

- The faith that everything will work out in my best interest even if I can't see it at this moment

- The knowledge that I'll have everything I need, including enough time

- Peace of mind and openness to experiencing larger realities

- The relief of being in the flow of life rather than struggling to make things happen

- Guidance to the right people and places to deliver my message

- The knowledge that I can trust in divine order

- The knowledge that I'm never alone

Something magical happens once we commit to allowing our divine selves to guide us. We begin to view the world through a pure, loving lens. We wake up and look for the evidence of the divine working in our lives and are able to focus on what's happening in the moment rather than projecting into the future or dwelling in the past. We look for opportunities to serve the greater whole and are willing to give up our righteous opinions and instead look for the gifts in every situation. When we are looking through divine eyes, we search for what's right about our lives and are grateful that we are alive and in a body—that we have the precious ability to think, feel, and make a contribution.

You'll know you are being guided by your divinity rather than your humanity when you stand in constant amazement at—and in awe of—your life and the universe. You'll feel connected and safe, and you'll trust that you will receive all that you need and all that you desire. You will feel entitled to the help and support of the universe and will watch in wonder as your heart's desires are fulfilled spontaneously and effortlessly.

So the big question is, What structure would you have to put in place today in order to choose a divine experience instead of a human experience? What support would you need to have in place in order to remember that you have a choice? What's going to remind you that the choice is yours every day? In the beginning of my process I used sticky notes that said, "Am I choosing from my humanity or am I choosing from my divinity?" I put them up in my car, carried them in my wallet, and posted them over my desk. Or I would have a daily call with a friend so we could support each other in choosing from the place of the divine. The point is, if we are going to do something out of the ordinary and live our lives from our highest state of consciousness, we must become present to the choices we make each day.

We all have the ability to access our divinity and share

it with the world. Coming from the perspective of our divinity means that we consciously access the highest place within ourselves before making choices that will affect ourselves, others, and the world. It means that we hold ourselves to a higher standard and are willing to give up our position. The value of this question is its capacity to make the unconscious conscious and give us access to perspectives and views that we were previously unable to see.

Asking this Right Question allows us to access the broader, more expanded version of ourselves even while we are living a human experience. What grander way to live life than to bring your beauty, sweetness, and magnificence to all situations? What greater gift can each of us give the world than to allow the divine to reign freely over our lives?

14

Living the Answers

Have you ever wondered what makes an extraordinary person? An extraordinary person is an ordinary person who makes extraordinary choices. Extraordinary people hold bigger visions for themselves than the ones dictated by their underlying commitments. They allow their individual lives to be used to serve the world around them. Extraordinary people make choices that are consistent not only with the highest expression of themselves but with the greater good of the world. If you closely examine the people you consider to be extraordinary, you will find that they are committed to excellence, to making a contribution, to not settling, to setting an example for others, and to taking the high road.

Each of us has this extraordinary potential. The promise of a flower lives within every seed, and within each of us lies the ability to lead an extraordinary life. But just as a seed needs sun and water in order to bloom into a flower, we too need nourishment and support if we are to blossom into our full magnificence. I promise you that by asking yourself the Right Questions and then taking the right actions you will make one extraordinary choice after another, choices that will allow you to become the person you were intended to be.

I began the miraculous journey of waking up to the totality of my humanity and my divinity almost twenty-four years ago. On the way to having the extraordinary life that I have today, I have devoted thousands of hours to seminars, lectures, books, and therapy. But truth be told, the thing that supported me more than any of those wonderful tools was the presence of a coach by my side. I once heard someone say, "No one gets to the Olympics without a coach, so why would you try to win your best life without one?" Wow, I thought, that seems so clear. Coaches act as our guides. They show us where we are, they hold a vision for where we want to go, and they support us in making whatever corrections we need to attain our goals. Everyone needs a coach, and everyone is entitled to one. I decided early on in my journey that I needed a coach if I was to bring forth the best possible life for myself and my family. I can honestly say that, since that time, I have never been without a supporting and guiding presence in some area of my life. Over the years I have had many different coaches—some friends, some professionals. They are everywhere we look for them. But they are only as useful as we allow them to be.

Today, my coaches make sure that I do exactly what I say I am going to do. They point out the blind spots in my own vision and show me where my next moves might be. My coaches are my champions. They are always in the background rooting for me and inspiring me to be as great as I can possibly be.

I certainly could not have gotten where I am today if I had gone it alone. I have by my side some of the most extraordinary people in the world. I surround myself with people who are dedicated to my vision and my highest good—just as I am to theirs—and who are relentless in their commitment to making sure I deliver the message I want to carry to the world. They stop me when I'm off course, they confront me when I'm being difficult, they love me when I'm scared, they applaud me when I'm brilliant, and most of all they inspire me to be the best me I can be.

So here is the final question I want to pose to you: What would you need to do to create a team around you to be your cheering squad? What would you have to create to make sure that no matter where you are in your life you have someone by your side who holds your highest vision in front of you and supports you in asking the Right Questions? Someone who champions you to make choices that are in direct alignment with your dreams for the future?

Getting this support does not require that you spend a lot of money. If you can't afford to hire an Integrative Coach or a life coach, you can gather people around you to support you in asking the Right Questions and making the right choices. You can ask a teacher or an admired friend to be your mentor, and you can return the favor to someone else. All you need is someone who will not let you compromise yourself or fall back into the patterns of your underlying commitments, someone who will hold you accountable for what you say you will do and who will remind you of your goals, even when you lose sight of them.

I hope you can see that the Right Questions are not about making that one big important choice, but about the small choices that you make all day long. The Right

Questions give you the power to make the higher choice for yourself at every moment of your life. If that's not what you're after—if you want to indulge in "poor me," if you're committed to being a victim and not going for all that you desire—then don't use these questions. But if you are committed to being the responsible creator of your reality, to being the best "you" that you can be, and to having your life make a difference, these questions will show you the way.

The Right Questions wake you up to the consequences of your choices and motivate you to take the higher road. It is only by questioning your automatic responses that you will break through the trance of denial and change routes. Ultimately you are the only one who can change the direction of your life. No one can do it for you. People can tell you again and again that you are headed down the wrong path, but until you see it for yourself, until you get tired of going around in circles, nothing will change. No one can choose the direction of your life—no one can make you take a particular path—but you. You get to decide: the path to nowhere or the path to the destination of your dreams—an extraordinary life. You choose.

Acknowledgments

I am blessed to have had the love, support, and assistance of many wonderful and talented people. There are really no words that can acknowledge what each of you brings to my life and work. While I cannot list you all, I owe my deepest and heartfelt thanks to a few people in particular.

To my sister, Arielle Ford, and her partner, Brian Hilliard, for being my dream makers. To Katherine Kellmeyer for being a sensational publicist and the entire staff of The Ford Group and Dharma Teamworks. To Danielle Dorman, thank you for all the ways that you contribute to my work, my life, and this book. Your thoughts, words, clarity, and unwavering commitment support me in more ways than you will never know. To the skilled and impeccable staff at HarperSanFrancisco—Liz Perle, my amazing editor and friend, Gideon Weil, Steve Hanselman, Marjorie Buchanan, Calla Devlin, Lisa Zuniga, Jim Warner, and Carl Walesa. Thank you for your commitment to excellence. My special thanks to Christopher Jasak at

Envie Salon and to Jeremiah Sullivan and Robert Bennett for once again making it happen. This book could not have happened without the care and expertise of each of you.

To the extraordinary Geeta Singh at the Talent Exchange for your dedication and devotion. To Justin Hilton, Cliff Edwards, and Jeff Malone for being accountable and brilliant. To Stephen Samuels, Anne Browning, Donna Lipman, Julia Aspinwall, Angela Delyani Hart, Beth Bennett, and the rest of my amazing staff at the Ford Institute for Integrative Coaching. Know that each of you inspires me and there would be no me without all of you. To David Goldsmith and Michael Greene of the Goldsmith Group for your expert advice and support in managing my business. And to the hundreds of certified Integrative Coaches who have dedicated yourselves to transforming lives and bringing this work to the world. Your commitment moves and motivates me. Thank you for sharing your lives with me.

To my many friends who are relentless supporters and contribute so much to my life and work: Gary Ravet for teaching me about extreme love, Cheryl Richardson for your laser, flawless coaching, Robby Lee for your tremendous guidance, Rachel Levy for always being my number one fan, Randy Thomas for bringing me the greatest gift of all, and Alanis Morissette for "getting my back." How lucky am I to have each of you?

To my beloved mother, Sheila Fuerst; my brother, Michael Ford; my earth angels, Kyda Kreizenbeck and Alisha Schwartz; and the rest of my family and friends for your endless love and support. To my son, Beau, and his two best friends, Stephen Wilkinson and Ryden Nelson, for showing me what true joy looks like.

To Ammachi for being an amazing teacher and a living example of service.

About the Author

New York Times #1 bestselling author Debbie Ford is an internationally recognized expert in the field of personal transformation. Her previous three books, *The Dark Side of the Light Chasers*, *The Spiritual Divorce*, and *The Secret of the Shadow,* have been translated into twenty-two languages and are used as teaching tools in universities and other institutions of learning and enlightenment worldwide. She is the founder of The Ford Institute for Integrative Coaching, a personal development organization that trains committed individuals with the skills, distinctions, and processes to facilitate a unique and impactful form of coaching. Hundreds of certified Integrative Coaches™ utilize Debbie's proprietary blueprint to support individuals in leading their greatest life.

Debbie's mission is to "inspire humanity to lead fully integrated lives." In addition to lecturing to conferences and groups across the United States and Canada, Debbie personally leads her acclaimed "Shadow Process Workshop," a profound three-day life-changing experience that inspires self-love and emotional freedom. Her Web site, www.debbieford.com, attracts thousands of visitors each month who are committed to producing extraordinary results through her numerous tele-classes, community calls, newsletters, and tape series. She is also the author of *The Right Questions in Action*, a bi-weekly coaching newsletter.